EXECUTIVE CHARISMA

EXECUTIVE CHARISMA

D. A. Benton

McGraw-Hill

New York Chicago San Francisco Lisbon London
Madrid Mexico City Milan New Delhi San Juan
Seoul Singapore Sydney Toronto

The *McGraw·Hill* Companies

5 6 7 8 9 0 DOC/DOC 0 9 8 7 6 5

ISBN 0-07-141190-9

McGraw-Hill books are available at special quantity discounts to use as premiums and sales promotions, or for use in corporate training programs. For more information, please write to the Director of Special Sales, Professional Publishing, McGraw-Hill, Two Penn Plaza, New York, NY 10121-2298. Or contact your local bookstore.

 This book is printed on recycled, acid-free paper containing a minimum of 50% recycled de-inked fiber.

Library of Congress Cataloging-in-Publication Data

Benton, D. A. (Debra A.)
    Executive charisma : how to win the job by communicating with confidence / by D. A. Benton.
        p. cm.
    ISBN 0-07-141190-9 (alk. paper)
1. Executive ability. 2. Executives—Conduct of life. 3. Executives.
4. Charisma (Personality trait) 5. Communication in management.
I. Title.
    HD38.2.B4622 2003
    658.4'09—dc21
                                        2003008123

To my husband, Rodney Sweeney,
and my parents, Fred and Teresa Benton.

And to the people who teach, help, and inspire me:
Mike Cohn, Amanda Mellos, Amy Zach Williams, Dr. Kelvin
Kesler, J. M. Jones, and all my clients . . .

Thank you.

Contents

Preface

GOOD LEADERSHIP TO GREAT LEADERSHIP

You've worked really hard to get where you are in life. You've studied, labored, gone the extra mile, taken on additional responsibility, continued your education, honed your instincts, developed sound judgment, retained your integrity, generated positive energy, dressed for success, achieved brilliance, and multitasked out the kazoo.

Because you've worked so hard, you've probably gained a certain level of leadership responsibility. This leadership responsibility has led you to embrace the ability to cope with change, deal with complexity, think strategically, organize and assemble a top-notch staff, analyze issues, anticipate trends, sense and set direction, plan, budget, and master problem solving (both yours and everyone else's).

Yet, despite all of that effort, you still haven't achieved the *significant* success, the level of accountability, impact, or influence that you want. The imaginary line on the wall where you want to "leave your mark" isn't high enough. As one person put it, "My name is not on the right door."

You're puzzled. What more can you do when you've done all you can? What you need to do is find the missing piece of the puzzle— the piece that turns you from a good executive into a great one.

The missing piece of the puzzle will be hard to find, and many give up and accept the fact that they will only achieve a certain level of success. But if you honestly strive to achieve the highest level of success, you have more work to do!

So what's the missing piece of the puzzle that will put it all together for you? It is *Executive Charisma.*

Before I tell you exactly what constitutes Executive Charisma and how you can get it, let me say a few words about what Executive Charisma is not. Executive Charisma is *not* selfishly ratcheting yourself up the ladder. It is not celebrity over leadership, not style over substance, not success over character. Nor is Executive Charisma some mysteriously seductive shaman/messiah mix. Executive Charisma is not magic; it is a skill that can be learned.

Executive Charisma is *the ability to gain effective responses from others by using aware actions and considerate civility in order to get useful things done.* While this definition may seem a bit nebulous, Executive Charisma is a tangible thing. You know "it" when you see it. You remember times when you have had this intangible thing yourself. You can think of people who have and use it well. Through their organized thinking and acting, they create passion and persuade people to their point of view.

"It's not just being charming, warm, and welcoming. It's a sense of confidence and a sense of personal ease that is overpowering and disarming, but not threatening to others. Charismatic leaders seem to have unique and meaningful insights into the business at hand and how selected individuals interplay with the critical issues involved," says Paul Schlossberg, CEO, DFW Consulting. "Understanding the business and the person makes them unique. That doesn't mean they are soft when it comes to standards. Normally, they are very tough in a positive way. They lead by competence because they're good at what they do and they lead by sheer effort in outworking everyone else. But they don't lead by fear."

Leaders with Executive Charisma possess that missing piece—popularly referred to at different times as interpersonal skills, shine, people skills, corporate chemistry, DNA, social currency, emotional energy, the unwritten code of behavior, or "fit."

"With [Executive Charisma] they are able to go into a whole variety of venues and be able to function at the top of their game," says Richard Torrenzano, CEO, The Torrenzano Group.

One venture capital partner said about Executive Charisma, "You have to face it, presentation is everything. You can be fantastic at your job, and achieve good results, but without presentation it's very limited. Great results can speak for themselves, but few truly achieve those on their own."

If you're in the corporate crowd at a C-level job (e.g. CEO, COO, CIO, CFO, CMO, CTO, CPO, CAO), or you want to be at that level, you need to get the missing piece. In addition to having the substance, as described in the first two paragraphs of this Preface, you'll need to have the style, too. You'll need to be memorable, impressive, credible, civil, clean-hearted, genuine, trusted, courageous, consistent, cool, calm, collected, confident, competent, comfortable, and, of course, charismatic.

With Executive Charisma, you raise your stock in yourself. You're inspiring. Executive Charisma helps you move easily in the world.

There has been a transformation in global business: How you work with people is as important as the work you do. Respect, purpose, goodness is required—in *addition* to achieving results on time and within budget.

In this book you will learn and understand what effective leaders do to build allegiance through *the ability to gain effective responses from others by using aware actions and considerate civil-*

ity in order to get useful things done. You will get "it" for yourself and, by your example, help others too.

"Finding a way to differentiate people across a large company is one of the hardest things to do," says Jack Welch, former chairman, General Electric. In addition to your substantive work contributions, that last piece to differentiate yourself is your Executive Charisma. It's the last growth area open to you when you've done all the results-oriented labor.

Over the last 10 years, as a practicing executive, I've studied this important part of leadership to (1) confirm its significance and (2) see how it's done. Using my database of detailed biographical and performance information of outstanding business executives around the world, as well as the *Fortune* and *Forbes* 500 and 100 lists, the *Inc.* 100 Top Entrepreneurs list, and so on, I identified individuals who are described as "leaders." And I identified comparative individuals who failed to get that label of "leader." I considered various "success" factors, including title, money, prestige, influence, power, respect from peers, private happiness, and personal satisfaction. I then studied the two groups to discover common variables that distinguished those who had an objectively successful life/career and those who didn't.

More specifically, I looked at how these executives think about themselves, about others, and about life. How they present themselves when content and not-so-content at work. How they deal with their own fears, concerns, and frustrations. How they try to go beyond dispensing information under the veil of communication but truly bond with people in a long-lasting interpersonal way.

From 1991 to 2001 I conducted more than 500 interviews with *the* "best" CEOs and key executives on how they do what they do.

I collected hundreds of articles and examined the new research in neurology, sociology, anthropology, psychology, and organizational development from Cornell, Rutgers University's Graduate School of Professional and Applied Psychology, University of Pennsylvania Graduate School of Education, Weatherhead School of Management, Daniels School of Business, Carnegie Mellon University, and others. And I compared patterns of findings from numerous leadership studies by the likes of PricewaterhouseCoopers, Accenture, Hay Group, Burston-Marsteller, and *Harvard Business Review*, among others.

I then synthesized the results to identify exactly what transforms hard-working, honest, earnest, skilled leaders *into* hard-working, honest, earnest, skilled, *effective and charismatic* leaders. In the final analysis every attribute of Executive Charisma was present in all of the "top" individuals, regardless of industry.

My goal in all this research was to find the missing piece of the puzzle for myself. Because, if you are like me, you were raised to believe that working hard, being smart, honest, and ethical is all that's necessary to get ahead. But what I've experienced tells me that although absolutely, undeniably *necessary,* hard work alone is not sufficient to achieve top success. This book was written to give you (and me) the necessary information to do well in substance *and* style.

My guess is that "substance stuff" comes easily to you anyway. Technical ability is often the simplest to acquire if you're bright. The difficult thing to master is the nuance of that intangible, illusive "it" factor. The soft stuff is the hard stuff. Just as you constantly work on getting better in the substance area, you also have to get better in the Executive Charisma area. If you're going to work on self-improvement, you might as well zero in on the right stuff to work on!

According to one study, "people skills" explain 85 percent of why we get, keep, and move ahead in our jobs. Our "technical competence" accounts for only 15 percent. In a different study of a diverse group of senior executives, three-fourths said interpersonal skills were the ones in highest demand and the ones most lacking.

In a thirty-five-year career you'll experience over 100,000 hours of decision making and 400,000 hours interacting with others (e.g., employees, customers, consumers, suppliers, shareholders, colleagues, managers, and other constituents). Every moment is another opportunity to practice and improve your Executive Charisma.

Super agent for celebrity athletes Mark McCormack says that one of the most toxic lies in business is that, "We judge people on their performance. If this were true the workplace would be a perfect meritocracy. The truth is more like, 'We judge your performance based on how much we like you.' People don't get fired for not doing their jobs well. They get canned because someone in authority doesn't like them. It's that simple."

Executive Charisma is something you have to have. Ideally it's an extension of your true personality and the natural outgrowth of having it all together. It has to be real, and it has to be visible. It is not a role that you play. You can't fake Executive Charisma, but you can embellish what you have. In other words, do what you're going to do anyway, just do it a bit better. And this book will help you.

As one man humorously put it, "Unfortunately this doesn't make you younger and sexier, add inches to your biceps or triceps, or instantly give you brighter and whiter teeth."

Executive Charisma will help you be described as a person who is sensitive and sensible, responsive and reflective, insightful and inspiring, instinctual and intellectual, comfortably confronting, transparently honest, sprightly and soft-spoken, tough, calm, and even-keeled; who has an easy smile, a calm demeanor, and a wry sense of humor, a contagious zest for life, a centered what-me-worry nonchalance, an at-homeness in his or her skin, a sharp competitive streak, and a lot of other cool things!

"I see a lot of incredibly educated, super smart people who lack street smarts and people skills. Some just don't get interaction on a personal level," says venture capitalist Gayle Crowell. "I invest in a person who is the morphine for business pain. You have to be able to attract customers, and have a reasonably profitable business model, but also be in the *buzz*. You want people talking about you, writing about you, and thought leaders quoting you."

People want a leader. Animals choose leaders. Preschoolers choose leaders. Gang members choose leaders. Workers choose leaders, but the leaders they choose aren't necessarily "the bosses." The leaders people choose to follow have "it." Jeff Cunningham, CEO, Cunningham Partners, Inc., says, "There is a primitiveness that we want in a leader: someone with warmth when you meet him, eyes that gleam, but who also holds everyone's feet to the fire including his own."

If after all this explanation it isn't "you" to use Executive Charisma, maybe you should try being someone else. Regardless of where you are in your career—to get things done and help people around you get things done—you can't waste any more time without it.

Executive Charisma is the last piece of the puzzle that you must figure out and apply. It's the best kept secret in business. And there is no walk of life where it doesn't apply.

Like you, other good people are providing the substantive content: hard work, energy, intelligence, instincts, and results. That's what makes them such formidable foes! When you pick up where your competitors leave off—improving your form and style with the last piece of the puzzle—you'll be the formidable rival to them.

Debra Benton
Benton Management Resources, Inc.
Fort Collins, Colorado

Acknowledgments

A special thanks to these people who generously offered their qualified opinion on the Sacred Six:

Carol Ballock, *Burson-Marsteller*

Thoko Banda, *deputy ambassador, Embassy of Malawi*

Andrew Basile, *partner, Cooley Godward LLP*

John Bianchi, *president, Frontier Gunleather*

Daryl Brewster, *group vice president, Kraft Foods*

Lynn Canterbury, *CEO, Horsetooth Traders*

Visda Carson, *partner, Accenture*

Curt Carter, *chairman and CEO, America, Inc.*

Bill Coleman, *founder/former chairman and CEO, BEA Systems*

Doug Conant, *president and CEO, Campbell Soup Company*

Cyril Cocq, *Ph.D., engineer, Altran Technologies*

Caroline Creager, *president, Executive Physical Therapy*

Mindy Credi, *vice president, human resources, PepsiCo*

Gayle Crowell, *partner, Warburg Pincus*

Jeff Cunningham, *CEO, Jeff Cunningham Partners, Inc.*

Pam Curtis, *president, Manfredo Curtis Consultants*

Jerome Davis, *president-Americas, EDS Business Process Management*

Bob DeWaay, *senior vice president, Bankers Trust*

Maury Dobbie, *president and CEO, MediaTech*

Greg Eslick, *president, ISTS*

Jack Falvey, *founder, MakingtheNumbers.com*

Athenia Figgs

Michele Fitzhenry, *vice president, TRRG*

Dale Fuller, *CEO, Borland Software*

Don Gulbrandsen, *CEO, Gulbrandsen Technologies*

Mark Gunn, *vice president, people, eMac Digital*

Cliff Hamblen, *president, Hamblen Sales*

Yvonne Hao, *McKinsey & Company*

Dave Hardie, *managing director, Herbert Mines Associates*

Kent Hayman, *CEO, ServiceWare Technologies*

Deb Hersh, *vice president, Home State Bank*

Kerry Hicks, *president and CEO, HealthGrades, Inc.*

Cathi Hight, *president, Hight Performance Group*

Adlai Howe, *vice president, Intraluminal Therapeutics*

Kate Hutchinson, *senior vice president, marketing, Citrix Systems*

Hal Johnson, *partner, Heidrick & Struggles*

Ragesh Jolly

Chet Kapoor, *vice president and general manager, BEA Systems*

John Krebbs, *CEO, PAC*

Natalie Laackman, *chief financial officer, eMac Digital*

Lawrence Land, *attorney*

Stephen Largen, *CEO, MacDermid Printing Solutions*

Pam Lawlor, *category leader, Quaker Oats*

Cynthia Liebrock, *president, Easy Access to Health*

Filemon Lopez, *vice president, Comcast*

Peter Mannetti, *partner, iSherpa Capital*

Reuben Mark, *chairman and CEO, Colgate-Palmolive*

Anne McCarthy, *dean, University of Baltimore, Merrick School of Business*

James Mead, *president, James Mead & Associates*

Nimish Mehta, *group vice president, Siebel Systems*

Steve Milovich, *senior vice president, human resources, The Walt Disney Company*

Michael Nieset, *partner, Heidrick & Struggles*

Kathleen O'Donnell, *partner, Advent*

Rick O'Donnell, *Colorado Governor's Office*

Cdr. Hal Pittman, *public affairs officer, U.S. Navy*

Gene Pope, *vice president, e-commerce platforms, Amazon*

Marc Robins, *founder, Red Chip*

Paul Schlossberg, *president, DFW Consulting*

John Slagle, *global market manager, General Electric*

Pat Stryker, *chairman, Bohemian Companies*

Richard Torrenzano, *chairman and CEO, The Torrenzano Group*

Michael Trufant, *CEO, ConnectUtilities.com*

Russ Umphenaur, *CEO, RTM Restaurant Group*

Chris Vargas, *CEO, F-Secure*

Cathinka Wahlstrom, *partner, Accenture*

Craig Watson, *CEO, Payment Engineering*

Mike Wilfley, *CEO, A.R. Wilfley & Sons, Inc.*

Wynn Willard, *chief marketing officer, Hershey Foods Corp.*

Ted Wright, *CEO, The Aslan Group*

Kal Zeff, *CEO, Carmel Companies*

EXECUTIVE CHARISMA

INTRODUCTION

The Foundations of Executive Charisma: Integrity, Confidence, and Full Disclosure

"You have to work at your leadership all of the time. You can learn to do it better, you can practice, you can nurture it, and you will do remarkably well," says Marc Robins, founder, Red Chip. "It's doing, not dash. It's not the car you drive, your wealth, your manicured look. It's keeping the right presence through the boring routine of being the kind of person everyone wants to look up to and who makes the decisions at the right time, all of the time. Executive Charisma, or personal magnetism, is like the bell curve. You want to be in the center and high. At the far left is temerity and at the far right, uncontrolled hubris. It's people who can integrate with other employees, associates, managers, executives, leaders, and service givers. It's the people who have the ability to draw on their temerity and hubris at the same time to relate, get to know, work, deal with, and confront people. Too often, people try too hard to create a façade that protects them and keeps others from seeing who they really are. That façade creates tremendous barriers in working with people. It's mostly driven by fear, ego, or unhappiness because these people don't know how to be any other way."

Integrity is essential. You have to be ethically sound. You really have no choice. I don't want to judge, preach, or appear self-righteous. In fact, I don't even want to talk about what should be the obvious. So do me a favor, if you have a "wavering moral compass," please stop reading. I'd rather you *not* know what I have to offer. Your integrity has to be consistent in all parts of your life. If you don't do what you say you will, or what you say doesn't add up, you have an integrity problem. Lack of integrity might not be repairable.

One female executive told me: "Taking credit for others' ideas is prevalent where I work. My associate, for example, she is really smart. I have to force myself not to take credit for her ideas even though I could do it and she couldn't do anything about it. She wouldn't even know. But I don't because *I'd* know. When I'm asked to do something unethical, which happens frequently, I just don't do it. Sometimes I tell them, 'This isn't something I'm comfortable with and this is what I'm going to do about it.' Sometimes I don't bother telling them I'm not going to do it. Later when they ask I tell them it wasn't right. Another thing that happens is the top people say they will do one thing when they know perfectly well they won't do it or they simply back out of it. I try to keep myself from not doing as they do. I'm at the point in my career where I'm really having to come to grips with what I will and won't do, despite what is apparently accepted."

To check up on your own integrity, ask: Am I doing what I promised? Have I done what I promised? Check yourself once an hour or, at the least, once a day.

Integrity, like morality and fairness, is often in the eye of the beholder. But you know yourself. You know whether or not you

- Tell the truth and don't stretch, distort, or come in late with it

- Live up to your word

- Worry about being "caught"

- Worry what your dad/mom or favorite mentor would think

- Would want your actions to be on the front page of your hometown paper

- Would be pleased and proud if your children behaved like you do

- Would stick with this approach even when it's inconvenient

"You can't talk yourself out of something you behaved into. You have to behave yourself out of it," says Doug Conant, CEO, Campbell Soup Company. "In my early career at Kraft we referred to the founder's guiding statement, 'What we say we will do, we do do.' If you start out on a slippery slope, your integrity will be forever questioned."

This is what I've learned about integrity from being around some of the best business leaders out there:

- The same show has to go on in front as on the "backside of the curtain."

- Your outward appearance has to show what's beneath the skin.

- Just because you don't like someone, doesn't mean the person lacks integrity.

- What goes around comes around more annoyingly.

- Don't expect people to be honest with you, if they're not even honest with themselves.

- You can't succumb to "incrementalism" (taking a little from the cookie jar, which goes unnoticed, so you take a little more, etc.).

- No one is completely worthless; a failure can always serve as an instructive example.

"The best chance you have of making it big is to decide from square one that you're going to do it ethically," says Alan Greenspan, chairman of the Federal Reserve Board. What quality is to a product, character is to a person.

Your integrity will give you confidence.

Confidence is a state of mind. Sometimes it gets shattered and you have to rebuild it. Sometimes you have confidence in one segment of your life but not in others. Confidence is not the absence of fear and apprehension; it's the conquering of it.

"People want confidence in their leader. You can't be a stammering, halting, doubting, individual," says Curt Carter, CEO, America, Inc. "You can worry that your plan won't work; sure, all good leaders do that. But you can't be worried if anyone likes you or not. You're like the rock in the river that the water rushes around. You have to look secure in yourself."

NASA flight director, Eugene Kranz, who was responsible for returning the crippled Apollo 13 spacecraft safely to Earth said, "You do not pass uncertainty down to your team members. No matter what is going on around you, you have to be cooler than cool."

Confidence can come from age and experience, upbringing, accomplishment, success, or money. This doesn't mean that all well-brought-up, successful, moneyed, older people have confidence.

Even President George W. Bush said after his election, "People are seeing whether I've got what it takes. You know who else is? *I'm* seeing whether I've got what it takes."

At one level, confidence is like integrity: You have it or you don't. Although you can't fake integrity, frankly you can fake a little extra self-confidence. Confidence is more conditional. Unlike integrity, it can waiver depending on the factors involved in a situation. Sometimes you just have more or less of it. We all do. That doesn't mean you can't act like you have more of it than you actually feel you have at any given moment.

A leader has to put on a "take charge" attitude, stand up straight, smile, and look people in the eye because a leader has to do the necessary results-oriented work. If you show confidence, people will treat you like you have the required confidence. If you don't act confidently, they'll treat you like you aren't.

People with integrity and confidence inspire both in others. Your apparent belief in yourself causes people to have more confidence in you. It creates a positive cycle when you bet on yourself and they then bet on you too.

Overconfidence that turns into arrogance will turn around and bite you. That is not what I'm promoting.

It's lifelong work to get, keep, and maintain internal confidence. And it's just as hard to display the external confidence that is necessary for both you and those around you.

"You have to talk about a problem like it's doable. You have to put on a game face earlier rather than later," says Daryl Brewster, group vice president, Kraft Foods.

One very successful CEO whose company is an industry leader and a legend told me, "Socially I've been relatively insecure ever since I was three years old. I was publicly laughed at because of something I said, and I've never gotten over it." He said this sixty years after the occurrence. Watching him in action you would never guess that. The truth about CEOs worldwide is that about 99.9 percent exude more confidence than they really have.

"You play the part before you get the part," says Deb Hersh, vice president, Home State Bank. "Lots of time you're out of your comfort zone, but you have to remember everyone sitting at the table has felt that. It's okay to feel anxious, but just go out and audition for the part."

With integrity and confidence (or display of confidence) you communicate and relate. The simplest, truest, and best way is with a full-disclosure approach.

Offering *full disclosure* means being direct, crystal clear, disarmingly open, and straight in all of your verbal and nonverbal communication. There should be no surprise, no mystery, and no deception in where you stand and what you think. With a full-disclosure approach you tell people your position, and you ask questions to get to know theirs.

People you work with are not mind readers. You can never assume they will understand your intentions. You cannot rely on innuendo.

Tell people what they need to know. Communicate early and often. With full-disclosure communication you take the mystery out of the relationship you're trying to build. You create a sense of accountability, which makes it very difficult to stray from commitments.

Tell people what you want or expect from them or what you plan for them. Ask what they want or expect from you and what they plan for you. Remove all fear, uncertainty, and doubt. It's unfair to expect people to know something without telling them what it is. It's the same as you learned in high school speech class: (1) tell your audience what you're going to tell them, (2) tell them, and (3) tell them what you told them. With clarity and focus explain the benefit (to both of you) in operating in a particular manner. If you don't disclose, you build a wall. Your openness, with a degree of humbleness, will build a bridge. (You have to do this whether your boss does it with you or not.)

The full-disclosure approach used by Steve Ross, former president of Warner Records, was "You come in, and if you've got a problem, you'll let me know. You don't have a problem and the company is running good, just keep going."

Bob Berkowitz, former White House correspondent, describes his use of full-disclosure communication, "What you see is what you get with me. I tell people who I am, what I'm about, what I do well, and what's important to me. At the same time I ask them who they are, where they are coming from, and what they want."

Doug Conant, CEO, Campbell Soup Company, says, "The first hour of the first day I work with someone, I declare myself. In that very first meeting, I say that my goal is to take the mystery out of our working relationship as quickly as possible, so that together we can constructively focus on the challenges at hand as early as possible.

"In that first meeting, I talk about what is important to me, what kind of leader I'm trying to become, what I value in an organization, what I look for in direct reports, how I believe our industry works, my planning philosophy, my operating style, my background, and my favorite quotes.

"At the end of the hour, I make the following point, 'I've just spent an hour sharing with you the way I intend to behave and some of the motivation for that behavior. If I do what I say I will do, I guess that means you can trust me. If I don't, I guess that means you can't. But I'm betting that you will find that I will do what I say I will do and that you can trust me, and that we can get on with the business at hand.' Also, I invite them to share with me, at a subsequent meeting, their personal philosophy as it relates to their work. Less than half take me up on it, but when they do, it really does constructively advance our working relationship."

Take a few minutes to write your own full-disclosure position as Berkowitz and Conant have. Think about the two or three things you want people to think about when they think about you.

"If you know their motive, character, and ability (and they know yours), you will be able to talk unfettered about behavior. This is the most important thing I know," says Curt Carter, CEO, America, Inc.

With the facts laid out you can address issues when problems arise. You don't point the finger, you ask. Whether it's a customer or a comrade you can say, "I remember this differently than you. Let's go back and see where we diverged."

As a leader, you must be disarmingly frank and have a no-non-sense ability to "get in the person's face" to forcefully lead, without being mean-spirited. Candor, decisiveness, rational aggression, execution, and a benevolent disposition when you hold the baton enable you to lead with a steady hand, not a rough hand.

You can be assertive, strong, firm in your convictions, tough, and resolute and still be pleasant in your perspective. You can say exactly what needs to be said, but you must say it in a way that you would want it said to you. You must pursue problems vigorously to deal with negative situations effectively and quickly. You must be direct, up front, matter-of-fact, frank but respectful, and tough but fair. That's a full-disclosure approach.

Ultimately your actions speak louder than words. You must live what you fully disclosed. The foundation for your Executive Charisma is integrity, confidence, and full disclosure. The Sacred Six Steps will help ensure that you live with integrity, confidence, and full disclosure.

These six steps are practical, successful trait-by-trait approaches that dissect the mind, deportment, and style of effective leaders. You and every progressive business manager must bring the Sacred Six into your skill base to deal with the challenges encountered in the real world. Your climb up the ladder will be quicker, more efficient, and certainly a lot more fun.

Wherever you are in life, you'll wish you'd started using these six steps years earlier. As Harvey Mackay, syndicated business columnist and author of *Swim with the Sharks* says, "Instincts alone are no match for this hands-on, heads-on information to fine-tune your best personal qualities."

"I've worked with company CEOs as well as presidents of the United States in my years at CNN, ABC, and NBC. The traits you teach are absolutely on target with what effective, successful leaders have," says Bob Berkowitz, former White House correspondent, author and host of the television talk show *New York Naked with Bob Berkowitz.*

THE SACRED SIX STEPS TO EXECUTIVE CHARISMA

1. *Be the first to initiate.*

2. *Expect and give acceptance to maintain self-esteem.*

3. *Ask questions, and ask favors.*

4. *Stand tall, straight, and smile.*

5. *Be human, humorous, and hands on.*

6. *Slow down, shut up, and listen.*

Using the Sacred Six Steps will help you

- Get done what needs to get done when it needs to get done and by whom.
- Control your effect on others versus leaving it to chance. Meet the "pattern recognition" the world has of a leader.
- Avoid self-sabotaging and career-derailing behavior.
- Send the message you intend to send about yourself.
- Set a good example and tone for others to emulate.
- Achieve staying power.
- Build and mobilize a vast network of followers.
- Create the reality that you want.
- Increase authenticity.
- Decrease invisibility.
- Work the "outside," and deal with the street, the media, and all of your constituents.

- Be at ease with people.

- Make your boss look good.

- Lift the fog of uncertainty from what works.

- Put yourself front and center as necessary.

- Increase differentiation.

- Set the standard for others to follow.

Whether it is a good or bad practice, people hire in their own likeness. If you want to work with a company that meets business needs, attracts customers, is profitable, impressive, trusted, ethical, strong, and in the buzz, then you'd better have these qualities too.

If you are in an organization that is none of those things, it will reflect on you. My advice is to get out. Morph into the kind of person you want to be and get in with a group of like-minded people.

You're here to take charge of your life and career—up the ante at crunch time. Don't do this to just survive, just to get by, or just enough not to lose. Don't do this if you just want a bigger paycheck and a more impressive title. Do it to win for you, your family, and your people. Do it to discover your life destiny.

You are the sum of the total of what you see, learn, and do. You are the only person who can help *you* with your life. As Mohandas K. Gandhi wrote, "You must be the change you want to see in the world. The best measure of what you will do is what you have done. Your past is your prologue."

I hope you'll feel like actor and producer Tom Cruise does, "I hate to go to bed at night thinking I didn't do all I could."

1

Be the First to Initiate

The United States did not rise to greatness by waiting for others to lead.

President John F. Kennedy

Your life is yours when you initiate. And your life belongs to others when you don't. The first step in Executive Charisma is taking the initiative in making the first move. If you wait until others do it, you might wait forever. There are *many,* many opportunities in your life just waiting to be seized. You can't let them go without a try. You have to take opportunities *before* you are ready, before you are invited, before you are comfortable, and before the ice is broken.

Counting the number of minutes in a day, you could say there are 1440 opportunities to start something. Even if you allow a generous amount of time for sleeping you still end up with well over 800 opportunities. Just think what might happen if you took one or two or ten more of those opportunities a day than you already do? Opportunities can be small and the results don't have to be perfect, but the opportunities do have to be initiated by you. Those opportunities are never lost. Someone else will take the ones you skip. So initiate exhaustively; don't hesitate.

One of the managers at The Palm restaurant in New York, which enjoys a "power meal" reputation, described the city's movers and shakers for me: "When they come in they go out of their way to be the first to introduce themselves, meet new people at a table, and to say hello to the wait staff. They acknowledge and greet everyone, including the ones they don't know." That's just one small way to initiate: talking to people you don't already know. Another way is doing what you've never done before.

Bill Coleman, the founder and former CEO and chairman of the board of BEA Systems took the initiative on a grand scale. Here is what he says: "There was a time in Silicon Valley that was a golden era and a golden place. You could fail at some venture and end up with a better job. It wasn't that you failed but that you took a risk, tried, learned from it and offered more value to someone else. I remember taking big risks thinking 'so what if it doesn't work, I would learn something.' At forty-five, when I started BEA, I could have stayed at Sun and made $10–20 million more. But I didn't want to be sixty and look back and wonder about what if I had."

You don't have to start your own business today, but you should take some actions outside your comfort zone. You can be pragmatic, focused, and mitigate risk, but you also have to take action.

You have to go beyond your comfort level in taking the initiative. If you wait until taking action won't be painful, you'll wait forever. Take heart in the fact that the pain is temporary but the change you make will be forever. Besides, trying new things only seems weird the first time. The greater the difficulty, the better a competitor you'll become, and the more you'll end up *enjoying* the glory.

A project manager of a hi-tech company said to me, "On Thursday I had several opportunities that I took with confidence as a result of your instruction. I want to tell you about one: I spoke with the COO of my company. Just walked up to him and expected acceptance. Well, you know what? I got it! As a result, I have a one-hour meeting scheduled with him next month to present an overview of a program I lead at the company. I've been waiting to have this opportunity for quite awhile as I believe he is the right sponsor. I kept waiting for my manager and my manager's manager to do it. It's been months. So, I did it myself. Took me about three minutes."

When you take the initiative you do something for yourself that no one can ever take away from you. One of my clients proudly told me the story of meeting the famous business guru Peter Drucker: "I went up, introduced myself, and we talked for ten minutes. That will always be a memory I made for myself and no one can take away from me."

An opposite example is the client who told me: "My sister is great at work but she doesn't want to take the first step. She wants to be discovered."

In taking the initiative, I'm not asking you to do like world championship cowboy Larry Mahan says about bull riding, "Take your brain out of your head and stick it in your pocket for awhile." I am asking you to accept the fact that the things I recommend you do will be uncomfortable and you will occasionally fumble. It's like professional BMX biker Matt Hoffman says, "The bad thing is you're going to fall; the good thing is, the pain will go away." You'll find out it's more like the owner of a trapeze school who says, "The first time you swing on the trapeze bar is for fear, the second time is for fun."

There may be situations where you'll feel very nervous, your hands will sweat, and your heart will throb. So what? Take a lesson from nine-year-old Chase Roubideaux when he met President Bush, "It's very special to meet the president, and sometimes you can just faint instantly. And I didn't want to faint because I thought it would be a waste of time."

It bears repeating: Your life is yours when you initiate. And it belongs to others when you don't.

HOW TO INITIATE

- *Put your fears aside or at least out of the way.*
- *Seize the moment; take some—almost any—action.*
- *Be consistent.*

Put your fears aside or at least out of the way. A little healthy fear is okay when taking the initiative so don't let fear hold you back. Too many great and fun opportunities are lost when you let people or situations scare you.

Sure you have a little inhibition about calling up senior people whom you don't know. But what do you have to lose? Nothing. So what if they don't take your call? They might! They aren't out and out rebuffing you. They just aren't interested in what you're doing, or they don't have the time to respond to you right now. If they rebuff you in a demeaning way, they, not you, have a problem. You should feel sorry for them.

We all can relate to the feeling that "if I didn't run away from my fears I'd get no exercise at all." However, you need to say to yourself with confidence, "I'm going to go and I'm willing to accept the consequences." Such an attitude is opposed to an arrogant attitude of "I'm going to go and I don't care about the consequences." The first statement is consistent with the Executive Charisma objective of gaining effective responses from others by using aware actions and considerate civility in order to get useful things done. The second one isn't.

To constantly apply all the aspects of your Executive Charisma is tough, but heck, you're a lot tougher. You'll end up with good memories and as one executive put it, you'll "kick butt too."

There are really two types of people in the world: those willing to take a risk and everyone else. Asking you to be courageous does not mean you have to eat grubs and junebug larvae, but courage does take effort and guts. "You have to risk losing the race to win it," says five-time Tour de France winner Lance Armstrong.

You might get embarrassed taking the initiative and maybe even get hurt. But like Winston Churchill said, "Nothing in life is so exhilarating as to be shot at without results." I picked up a greeting card once with a message that stuck with me. It read, "If you're going through hell, keep going."

Relish risk, at least occasionally, because if you never take it, you'll never know what you can do. Take big risks too; small ones aren't worth the calories they burn up.

Seize the moment; take some—almost any—action. The one or two or ten minutes it takes to do what terrifies you the most can determine the rest of your life.

Your success, happiness, future, and fortune depend on your willingness to initiate. The late Malcolm Forbes wrote: "You alone can move your own legs. You alone can utilize your hands. You must stand on your feet, physically and metaphorically. You must take your own steps. You must govern your own tongue. You have to dig your own monument or your own pit. Which are you doing?"

One of your 800 or more moments in a day could be used to

- Talk to a total stranger you meet at the grocery store or office cocktail party as if you already knew them. Give them the same warmth, humor, and "personableness" that you'd give a longtime friend.

- Send a handwritten congratulatory note to an important or interesting person you'd like to get to know.

- Telephone the person you met on the airplane to thank him or her for that excellent restaurant recommendation. Offer to return the favor with a similar recommendation in your city.

Taking initiative can be very politically savvy; as Barbara Bush advised Laura Bush, "Be sure to be the first to shake hands with the wives of your husband's foes."

Dick Werth has a used car dealership in Hays, Kansas. If you visit his home office, you see an impressive array of framed autographed photos from the likes of Frank Sinatra, Jimmy Carter, George Bush, Sr., Ronald Reagan, George Burns, Jimmy Stewart, Gerald Ford, Bob Hope, Walter Matthau, Jack Nicklaus, and Jack Lemmon. Why? Because he initiated contact by writing to them and they responded.

Every day (even on vacation days) target someone with whom you can initiate a greeting, a question, or a conversation. One current buzz expression is to "think outside of the box." Well, you can "*go outside of the box*" too. Stop and chat up some person you regularly see but have only exchanged "hellos" with. Find out where he's going on vacation, where his son goes to school, what he did before his current job, and so on.

There are hundreds of ways to test your limits! I know one man who keeps a piece of paper in his shirt pocket. As he meets new people during the course of the day, he puts each person's name on the paper. At night he looks at that piece of paper and gives himself a little "bonus" for every name on it. Obviously if it's blank he didn't seize opportunities and he doesn't get a bonus! While you're trying new things it's good to keep a personal scorecard. If you don't make a mental and physical note, you won't always remember how much you've done (or haven't done!) and what you've improved upon.

The idea is to get you out of the box to (1) practice the skill of initiating so it becomes your habit; (2) learn or experience something new; and (3) get out of the rut, break old habits, and try something different. If you get rejected when you initiate (e.g., someone ignores you, is brusque in tone, seems bothered by your intrusion, walks away in a huff, or gives you a dirty look), so what? It's that person's loss. Move on and initiate a conversation with someone else! There isn't a right way or a wrong way to initiate—the important thing is to do it! But there are some guidelines you can follow and one guideline you *must* follow:

Be consistent. You know you need the will to accomplish new things, but what really makes the difference is having the discipline to keep trying. You'll find that what "they" say you can't do doesn't apply to you because you never stop or give in.

Keep a piece of paper in your pocket, reward yourself with a dollar bill in a mason jar, and keep your personal scorecard. It's basic goal setting. But *do it* and do it all of the time whether you feel energized or not. The response you get may be just what you need to get revved up.

When you initiate, don't be disappointed in others' reactions. Even when you do everything right, there are some people who won't react and respond the way you wanted or hoped. Don't get frustrated or give in to despair. Plant your feet, take the initiative, and try again. As NFL coach Mike Ditka says, "You never really lose until you quit trying."

The ad copy for an athletic shoe sums it up, "Gear up and get out." That's pretty much what you have to do now. Everything you'll learn about Executive Charisma in this book is just the beginning. It takes you to execute it. Do whatever you choose to do, just don't get caught waiting.

Fearlessly seizing the moment *only occasionally* isn't sufficient. You can't allow circumstances to dictate when you can waiver from your objective. You need to be the first to initiate all of the time with everyone, and you have to keep at it. It has to be like breathing. Do it when you're mad, glad, sad, happy, energized or not. It's one of those differentiators Jack Welch spoke of in the quote included in the Preface.

"Successful people have a proactive trait," says Gayle Crowell, partner, Warburg Pincus. "More often than not they'll initiate. Instead of waiting for things to happen they make them happen first. If I wait it will never happen. There is a fair amount of risk and rejection to be ahead of the curve. But the percent of risk is higher if you don't."

Every moment is another chance for you.

2

Expect and Give Acceptance to Maintain Esteem

Expecting and giving acceptance to maintain esteem must be your mental mode of operation to execute your Executive Charisma. It's the gauge you stop at and check and plan your action against. Without this component *any* move you take to control your effect on others can end up as a manipulative, scheming, and game-playing trick. That is not what this book is about.

As a human being walking this Earth you have a right by birth to expect acceptance from everyone and you have an obligation to give it to everyone. You can't expect it for yourself and not give it to others. Success in your Executive Charisma is a direct result of consideration of others' esteem as well as your own.

If you don't expect acceptance, you won't get any. If you do expect it, you just might. One CEO told me, "I always ignore the color of skin, but I never ignore whether they expect acceptance from me or not."

Forget your blushing, sweating, trembling, and shaking as you expect and give acceptance. Ignore the heart palpitations from dealing with intimidating people, the embarrassment in talking to strangers, the fear of authority, or the possibility that someone may criticize you.

Erase thoughts such as *"I got here totally by accident and I'll be found out." "I'm dreading the day when someone is going to get me for that." "I'm close to being found out so I'll hide out where I am."*

If you give acceptance to others, they just might live up to it. If you don't give it, they'll show you! You can't pick and choose to whom you give acceptance. You cannot mentally position people negatively. You must accept people as they are, not as you would like them to be. Practice the golden rule. If you give people close to you courteous attention, give the same courteous attention to strangers. Give people whom you think you won't see again the same treatment that you give those whom you will.

"A person can be an ally or foe down the road; it all depends on how you talk to them. I learned that growing up in the construction business with my dad. The secretary you're dealing with today could be the wife of the contractor you have to deal with two weeks from now," says Gene Pope, vice president, e-commerce platforms, Amazon.

"I can't give more money but I can give respect," says Mark Gunn, vice president, people, eMac Digital. "You can't give it if you don't have it for yourself. I give unconditional respect. Respect is like love, you can't have boundaries on it. When you give respect it's hard for people to turn around and treat you badly."

The *Harvard Business Review* featured research by Robert Goffee, a professor at London Business School, and Gareth Jones, a professor at Henley Management College ("Why Should Anyone Be Led by You?"), which found: "Leaders produce within them three emotional responses. The first is a feeling of significance. Followers will give their hearts and souls to authority figures who say, 'You really matter,' no matter how small the follower's contributions may be. . . . The second is a feeling of community [defined by them as a group that has a unity of purpose around work, and, simultaneously, a willingness to relate to one another as human beings]. . . . Finally, followers will tell you that a leader is nearby when they get a buzzing feeling. People want excitement, challenge, and edge in their lives. It makes them feel engaged in the world. And so despite all the literature that tells you a leader needn't be charismatic, followers will sooner feel leadership from someone who is extroverted and energetic than from someone who isn't. Right or wrong, that's how followers feel."

Note the first emotional response: feeling of significance. Isn't that what you want? Well it's what everyone else wants too, and that's what expecting and giving acceptance to maintain self-esteem is about.

A CEO told me about his recently promoted president: "He expects to be treated as an equal by the board of directors, by Wall Street, by the community at large. Even when he was a first-line supervisor he was like that. Because he expects it for himself he consequently treats everyone else that way too. He's never taken a subservient position. He's never had his hat in hand to be recognized, nor crawled on his knees even if he was meeting the Queen. His body language is so subliminal he's not even aware of it. He brings his own agenda and doesn't wait to say something first. In a nice, proper way he's definitely willing to state his disagreement. He respects a person's service, age, experience, and knowledge. He treats everyone as an equal. He knows everyone is different but not better." That's why he was promoted.

There will always be new players and different rules in any situation you are in, in any part of the world. If your starting point is always to expect and give acceptance, you'll be able to figure out what's required.

EXPECT ACCEPTANCE

Expecting acceptance is putting yourself on par with any other member of the human species. Expecting acceptance is stubbornly and justifiably holding a belief of simple self-acceptance. No one is above *or* below you. You are all at the same level.

Obviously, to expect acceptance means to cease downgrading yourself, to cease feeling unappreciated, disappointed, cynical, vulnerable, hopeless, helpless, or of low self-esteem. As mentioned, any misguided attitude of "I'll be found out . . . I'll be exposed" has to stop.

Instead, you have to initiate a conscious, deliberate, persistent attitude of expecting acceptance from other humans regardless of whether they earn more money, carry a loftier title, or appear to have more power, experience, status, and so on. You're all standing on the same stage; no pedestals are allowed.

The Ritz-Carlton hotel group teaches each new employee their "Gold Standard" service policy, part of which is the corporate motto: *"We are Ladies and Gentlemen serving Ladies and Gentlemen . . .*

we are service people not servants." Ritz-Carlton customers and employees are equals in term of human dignity. That mission statement exemplifies perfectly the attitude of expecting acceptance.

We all do practice expecting acceptance *sometimes.* When you get behind a steering wheel in an automobile, for example, don't you automatically feel equal on the road to anyone else in a car? Cars are a great equalizer. If the speed limit is 70, you go 70. If someone tries to get in the lane in front of you, it's like "Katie, bar the door." The vehicle shell makes you feel as though you own the road. Title, power, and social status no longer matter. Put two tons of steel in your hands and you're a superperson. But step out of the car, and the mantle of power falls from your shoulders. If you feel on par on the road, you should also feel on par in life. Expect acceptance on the road of life as well as on the highway road.

Everyone knows people who can intimidate, overwhelm, rankle, derail, or overly impress. They are found in your church, community, company, association, and neighborhood. People don't have power over you unless you give it to them. Don't let them do that to you. My dog, Scooter, will "sit" for me on command, but if the president of the United States told him to sit, Scooter would just give him the paw because he doesn't give the president power over him.

You mentally protest, "Yeah, but I'm just average . . . what right do I have to expect acceptance?" The answer is *every* right. Hopefully, here's some "mental comfort food" for you: We're *all* typical average blokes just trying to get along in life. Besides, you can be average and still feel respect for yourself and have trust in your ability.

Expecting acceptance doesn't mean you cease giving the respect, attention, and appreciation due to individuals who have "power" in your life (e.g., bosses, elders, public officials, law enforcement personnel). You can have a strong sense of your own shortcomings and at the same time still expect acceptance for yourself. Too many times you easily and readily give acceptance to others but *not* to yourself. I have to ask you: If *you* won't, who will?

I know that some social upbringings might cause you to put yourself down in order to show respect to others. But that kind of thinking needs to be changed. You can give respect to others while simultaneously giving it to yourself.

A first-time manager I coached told me, "I understood intellectually what you were saying, but it took a few months to start behaving and believing it myself. I'm transformed—both in my life and my work. I am more calm and less fidgety, I exude more self-confidence, and, in general, finally I am letting the world see me."

You should expect acceptance not to increase your popularity or to prove you "belong" or for friendship. It's not the long-remembered Sally Field Oscar acceptance speech of "You like me. You really, really like me." Nor is it an overdeveloped sense of entitlement where you are owed something. You aren't. Expecting acceptance is not seeking approval. You (or me or anyone else) will never get all that you (or we) want.

Here's one executive's testimonial to the power of expecting acceptance: "I was invited to a lunch at a local old-boys club. I expected to be part of a large anonymous gathering. I show up at a small board room table for 12, and as soon as we sit down the chair asks us to introduce ourselves and speak briefly about our work, life, and what excites us. All my insecurities come bubbling up as my turn comes around and the sweat starts pouring down my back! I mean, these guys are really important and I feel like a total imposter. To make a long story short, I remind myself that they invited me here for a reason, activate my Cheez Whiz™ smile, remind myself that I am as adequate as anyone else in the room, and leave very pleased with my modest statement."

The amazing thing about acceptance is that many times people will give you more than you'll give yourself. On his last day as GE's chairman, Jack Welch was interviewed on the *Today Show* and was asked "What was your secret of success?" Welch said, "Always hiring people smarter than me." Now Welch is reportedly pretty smart and, despite recent events, one of the most successful CEOs ever. Yet he says, at least publicly, that he hires people smarter than himself!

Interestingly, that's a comment I hear all of the time from CEOs. Strong leaders in all walks of life report that they "hire smarter and better" than themselves. My advice to you is, "Live up to their acceptance!" If you don't give it to yourself, why would they want to give it to you? You're insulting them. At the very least, you are discounting their judgment, and definitely wasting a lot of everyone's time.

The director Woody Allen puts his comedic spin on surrounding himself with good people, "Hire the best. Get out of their way. Then come in and take credit for their work."

CEOs hire smart, but they expect you to know it and act it without a lot of reinforcement, constant approval, or public recognition. You'd better have your act together around people with a few more stripes on their sleeve than you. If you walk around with an intimidated attitude of "Ooh, my God, ooh, my God" around them, you'll fail their test. To pass the test, courageously expect acceptance.

"I'm astounded how many high-powered people are more than will-ing to give you a chance to play with them. People who have confidence, security, and charisma are very open to others who have it too," says Peter Mannetti, partner, iSherpa Capital. "The people you want to emulate are most apt to accept you for who you are when you expect acceptance."

An antiviolence group, Safe Child, distributes a list of charac-teristics found in bullies. "They have a need to feel powerful; derive satisfaction from inflicting suffering on others; have little empathy for others; defend their actions by blaming others; and are generally defiant and antisocial."

Those characteristics are just the opposite of those of someone who expects acceptance.

Bullies can tell immediately whether you are a target and whether they are going to try to mess you over. There are plenty of people in life who live by the motto: "If you can be taken advantage of you're fair game." One man put it, "The more crap you put up with, the more crap you are going to get."

If you still choose not to expect acceptance you'll get your wish. You'll live up to your low expectations since your low expectations are high enough for you.

If you think or act like you are a substandard human being, you'll be treated as one. If you surrender your value, you are at the mercy of anyone's will. Remember this: Supplicants don't get respect, they get pity, get ignored, and get dismissed.

Expecting acceptance is a new level of empowering yourself in how you think, act, and relate. "Recognize that with every decision you face, you have the power to choose your response. Between the stimulus and the response there is a space. In that space is the power of choice," says Doug Conant, CEO, Campbell Soup Company.

HOW TO EXPECT ACCEPTANCE
- *Tell yourself, "I'm adequate."*
- *Behave as though you expect acceptance.*
- *Keep at it even when you don't get it.*

Tell yourself, "I'm adequate." All day long when you aren't talking to someone else, you are talking to yourself, and the amount of negative self-talk is shocking. One person called it "his self-beclouding." Stop it. If someone else were saying those same things about you, you'd be royally miffed. Even if the negative stuff were true, you have a right to change your mind and change your action.

"I'm adequate" self-talk is a start. If you don't say "I'm adequate" you're by default saying "I'm inadequate" and undeserving of acceptance. That's just not the case. Adequate doesn't mean satisfied, settled, content, or resigned though.

I know being adequate doesn't sound grand or high enough, but it is the highest level you can aspire to. Think about it. If you tell yourself you're *in*adequate, you're not likely to expect acceptance. You'll look and act like you don't deserve it. If you live that way, people will conclude that you don't deserve acceptance and won't give it to you. Then you end up feeling resentment for not getting it. (Self-help gurus call this a self-fulfilling prophecy.)

Saying "I'm adequate" does not translate to "I'm average." (You're above average just because you're reading this book.) It's telling yourself "I'm okay," "I'm capable," "I will prevail," and "I'm fully up to any task." You are the best form of yourself when you feel adequate. You're a "player," you make a difference, you actualize yourself, you'll step beyond boundaries—in a humble, not elitist, way.

One CEO told me, "The older I've gotten and the more I've done the more adequate I feel."

I know being "adequate" still may not sound that good, but it is if you view it as the opposite of being "inadequate." A man once said to me that 75 percent of the people in corporations are adequate, implying that they just punch the time clock. I said, you're wrong, 100 percent are—meaning there aren't 25 percent inadequate or super-adequate people.

You aren't *in*adequate even if you tell yourself you are, but for goodness sakes, stop feeding your brain trash talk. Manage your thoughts instead of leaving them mismanaged. A mantra of "adequacy" helps you avoid the emotional bungee jump you put yourself through when you deconstruct your day. In life, there are few things you have control over: Your attitude toward yourself is one of them. As the author W. H. Auden said, "A man is known by the company his mind keeps."

I'm not suggesting denying reality or the need for personal and professional development. We all have that need. Stop focusing on your imperfections alone. You *are* adequate as a human being who is also a boss, an employee, a spouse, a parent, a friend, and so forth. When an area pops up that you need to get better in you should say to yourself, "I'm adequate (as a human) but am working on getting better at . . ." versus "I'm not good at . . . and I'm a loser too."

Please note that this self-talk is not a reckless chirping or a syrupy motivational cheer of "I am good. I am great." It is thinking and saying to yourself, "I am adequate, I won't feel inferior, *and* I want to get better." Your brain (and other people) believes what you tell it. Tell your brain what you want to register; tell it where you're going, not where you've been.

On average you have 50,000 thoughts a day. It takes intense concentration and persistence to manage those thoughts. Researcher Thomas Crook, president of Psychologix, proved that after 35 years of age, on average we lose 1 percent of our brain volume each year. (And that doesn't account for the brain cells lost through extracurricular activities!) Better make sure the part that remains is in control with "I'm adequate" self-talk.

Behave as though you expect acceptance. If you act as though you belong where you are, doing what you are doing, no one will question you and you'll get the support you need. Take a minute and reflect on some encounter that went well. You probably expected acceptance—and got it. Think about an encounter that went wrong. You probably didn't expect acceptance—and you got it.

Suffice it to say, if you feel it, think it, but don't show it, it is all for naught. People believe what they feel. They call it their intuition, gut feeling, sixth sense. And they feel it based on what they see.

Forest Glazer is fresh out of college into a new job dealing with colleagues much older and more experienced. I asked him how he shows that he expects acceptance. "I tuck my shirt in. Look 'em in the eye. Shake hands. Talk matter of fact in a down-to-earth manner."

As MediaTech CEO Maury Dobbie describes the acting, "It's looking face-to-face, straight in the eye, taking the edge off your voice, eliminating a defensive attitude and as the cliché goes: never let 'em see you sweat."

I think of an acquaintance in a wheelchair. He says that what he misses most is the ability to look at people face to face, at eye level. From the chair he always has to look up to people, and they have to

look down on him. Inventor Dean Kamen solved that physical obstacle with a motorized wheelchair that has a special feature called the
standing mode. The machine rises up on its wheels and lifts its occu-
pant to eye level while maintaining perfect, stable, unshakable balance. As Kamen says about people who've tested it, "It brings tears
to their eyes when they can stand up and make eye-to-eye contact."

Most of us do not have such a disability. So why handicap yourself by sitting in a mental wheelchair and not feeling "eye to eye" with
people. That's all expecting acceptance is about.

Gayle Crowell spends a third of her time interviewing people.
She's evaluating track record, skill set, and Executive Charisma. It's
not enough for the individual to be able to do a deal or build a company. "To be a sustainable model I have to be able to visualize him
sitting in front of a CEO and capturing his attention," she says. "With
Executive Charisma you own the room; without it you don't."

Let me describe Crowell and others who have Executive
Charisma. They are bright and knowledgeable about "their game."
They seem content with the value they bring. They are incredibly
direct—not harsh and abrasive, but clear. They select what needs to
be said and done. They are aware of the audience and what's important to it. People are interested in them because they are confident,
stand tall, walk around, and are the first to shake hands or hug. When
you talk to them, you feel as though you're the only one in the room
even if there are a hundred people there.

"I expect people to react positively. I show great interest in
them—as individuals and in their concerns. I expect them to like me
and want to work with me. I am going to make an impact. People meet
my expectations because I'm very clear about them going in," says
Steve Milovich, senior vice president, The Walt Disney Company.

Your expectations create a positive cycle. You expect acceptance; you get it. You do better; they are reinforced in giving it. They give more; you do better. The cycle doesn't stop.

Behavior sent "out" sets up expectations of behavior sent "back." Cool, distant, aloof gets sent out; cool, distant, aloof comes back.

Your behavior has to constantly corroborate your attitude. Your attitude has to be one of expecting acceptance from anyone, at any time, anywhere. The toughest time to do it is when others don't do it and that's the most important time to do it.

Keep at it even when you don't get it. Now, as much as I promote your expecting acceptance, I'm not so naïve as to realize that you won't *always* get it. This happens. (Well, it happens a lot, unfortunately.) Despite your good effort there will be "infractions" of your rules of expected behavior.

If someone "does you wrong," deal with it early, not later. As Mark Gunn suggests, "Go to them. Find out where they're coming from. If it's different than what you think, find out what can be done about it. Tell them where you're coming from—both always done with respect."

I've found there are basically two types of people who don't give acceptance. The *first* type refuses to outwardly give acceptance to you, even when you "expect" it because these individuals are themselves insecure. Notice I said "outwardly" give acceptance to you. Truth is, they may actually be giving acceptance to you, but because of their own character flaws or personality disorders, are afraid to show it. They're going to treat you poorly, test if they can get away with it, and try to discourage you from coming back with self-acceptance. If they discover that they can bully you, they'll continue to do so.

The *second* type who refuses to outwardly give acceptance to you does it to make you stronger. Such a person can be called your "friend." Many who care about you won't readily give acceptance to you in order to make you work harder to develop the skill of self-acceptance. If they make it difficult for you, you'll learn to work to overcome the obstacle, and hence get stronger and better.

Regardless of the reason for their behavior, you handle it with the same dos and don'ts.

Do initiate expecting acceptance. If you don't start out with that attitude (and keep it up) you'll never get it. It all has to start somewhere, and it might as well be with you. If you wait until you get it first, you might wait for a very long time.

Don't try to give them "some of their own medicine" by ceasing to give them acceptance while expecting it for yourself. Don't snub, ignore, or put them down. If you retaliate in kind, you will not feel better about yourself later, nor will you "win." As one executive said, "Never argue with idiots. They drag you down to their level, and then they beat you up with experience." Plus, the only thing you accomplish is getting riled up in your own fury.

Maury Dobbie, CEO, MediaTech, told me about a difficult meeting with a group of men, where the leader was resisting her proposal and giving her grief in general. "I just took a deep breath and mirrored the guy. I gave it right back in a friendly, humorous, direct way. I honored his opinion and position but stood firm in my own also. We got the contract. Later one of the other men in the meeting met me in the hallway and said 'You did great. He was just trying to test you.'" Maury added, "It's fun to earn their respect."

One CEO told me he'll "throw a curveball" for sport, out of boredom, and "because I can." He even admitted, "Sometimes I do it because I'm attracted to the person!"

When you are faced with a test,

- Keep acceptance going anyway.

- Care less about the opinion and more about whether there is a kernel of truth.

- Don't get defensive.

- Ask about the critique.

- Probe about the person's motivation.

- Remember, it's more about the other person than it is about you.

- Don't get even.

- Find the humor in it.

- Challenge the person in a gentle way.

Look inward too. Was it a misunderstanding on your or the other person's part? Did you deliver the message correctly? Is the outcome realistic? Why didn't it go as planned?

Deb Hersh, vice president, Home State Bank, gives herself a little talk, "I ask myself why I feel this way; then I interject a positive thought, and remind myself that fine pottery and fine metal has to go through fire."

Another person says, "I make the difficult people my project. I throw energy and attention their way so when we finish they wonder why they ever gave me any trouble."

Don't "give in and go along" even one iota when others pull their first "power play." You will never regain respect, and they will continue to abuse you even more. They must learn *from the start* that they can't get away with that behavior toward you. You won't react and go away like the others. And if you've already let people "do it to you," now is the time to correct the situation by using what you're reading in this book. Regardless of the outcome, you'll feel better about how you handle yourself.

Don't whine, pout, or complain about not getting acceptance. Do get creative in how you turn the tide though. See it for what it is, assess the situation, dismiss your emotional hurt, and try a new approach. At the very least you confuse the power players because you are not like most people, whimpering away into the corner. Pre-think different approaches before things go wrong. Even if you don't have to call on your alternative plans, you have them. That alone affords you less uncertainty and fear, and your pre-thinking might even prevent a problem in the first place.

Above all, don't let these power players change your approach. Confuse them in your nonreactive, pleasantly assertive manner. Treat them as if you *are* getting it from them.

The more they push and the more you pleasantly and assertively fight back will be in direct proportion to their eventual respect of you. They will recognize that you are different and that their destructive style will not work with you at all. If their motivation was to test, you'll pass; then they will treat you as a peer and welcome you into "their circle." If a person's motivation stemmed from his or her own insecurity, it remains for that person to come to grips with his or her internal issue.

Unfortunately, there are too many people in this world who seek to defeat you by defeating your self-acceptance. If you allow yourself to be bothered by their nonacceptance instead of doing something about it, you lose and they win.

Take consolation in the foolishness of those who don't see and value you as they should. Sacrifice your emotional hurts from the initial sign of any disturbance, confrontation, or stress. You'll find that since you're on the right track you'll be able to bear anything. As one person said, "I just laugh it off, forget about it, and go and get a foot massage."

You can do it *all* right and still receive in return bold-faced, neon-lighted, negativism/rejection. There are some people I call "human car wrecks." You can't avoid them. Like in a car, you can wear your seat belts, obey traffic laws, look both ways, and still have someone crash into you. A client described such a person, "I thought I was doing things right and well and she 'broadsided' me with her approach. In fact, she backed up and ran over me again." Hopefully, you don't meet too many of this type of person in your life—either literally or figuratively. There will be times in your life that you deal with someone who is such an empty suit, so full of nothingness, that you just have to do like you do with your TV remote: Shut it off and walk away. (And get that foot massage.)

Despite all your gracious, good effort there will be some people you will not want to deal with in the future. They are so insecure in themselves, so afraid, or so downright mean and misguided that they aren't just a car wreck but a train wreck.

Nonetheless, even with them, you start out giving acceptance. And you keep giving it until they absolutely, positively, categorically, and repeatedly prove to you alone that it's best to walk away. Expecting acceptance is necessary particularly when you are around people who don't normally give it, don't know how, or don't want to.

Sometimes you are given too much "acceptance" because of your title, power, and so on. When that happens:

- Give acceptance back in kind.

- Don't take advantage of acceptance.

- Don't get "taken" with yourself.

Don't think you are owed acceptance. Instead, use acceptance to put people at ease around you. Acknowledge, show interest, and give back.

To minimize the halo effect he gets because of his status, one CEO I know goes into a room "under the radar." He goes around and talks, meets people one on one, and gathers information before they find out who he is and get intimidated.

If you are an intimidating presence, you can revel in it or you can use it productively to get useful things done in a civil manner through people. Start by giving acceptance, continue by utilizing all the components of Executive Charisma as laid out.

GIVE ACCEPTANCE

Expecting acceptance is necessary. Giving it is just as necessary. There is no way around it, and there is no exception to the rule.

Giving acceptance is to acknowledge one's presence, one's contribution, one's ability, and one's existence. People need verbal, nonverbal, or emotional validation. The worst insult is to ignore. Because the need for acknowledgment is strong, people would even prefer you fight with them than ignore them. Some do silly things even though they are made fun of in an attempt to avoid invisibility. From childhood on they learned to get attention one way or another—passively or aggressively.

Older people will tell you one of the frustrations with age is that it makes you invisible.

Giving acceptance starts with acknowledgment—symbolic and real: a word, a nod, a look, a smile, a touch to authenticate the person. Giving the correct, instinctive consideration that others deserve follows. It is the same consideration that you deserve.

You have an obligation to cultivate a genuine acceptance of people as they are. Most are fine and capable people, intelligent, efficient, and effective enough for most situations. And for those who are marginal, your support might mean the difference they need. Treat others as you want to be treated—with respect and honor. If you want a "100 percent fair shake and clean slate," you have to give it to others. You give a "second chance" the same way you want a second chance. You're as tolerant of others' failings as you want them to be tolerant of yours. You don't pick and choose whom you give it to. You give everyone permission to operate on the same plane as you. If you don't give acceptance, this whole Executive Charisma thing won't work for you.

"Acceptance is simply conscious empathy. It's really trying to put myself in the other person's shoes," says Kerry Hicks, president and CEO, HealthGrades.

When you give acceptance, you make people comfortable around you because they trust someone who accepts them. When people are comfortable, they often break through limits imposed by their own fears and doubts. You help them achieve something more than they thought possible because you

- Help them maintain their own self-esteem

- Increase their sense of worth

- Enhance their personal dignity

- Maximize their well-being

Giving acceptance is not falsely lifting up others, saying whatever anyone wants to hear, not personality worship, apple polishing, or absurd adulation. It's just a neutral or positive attitude toward others versus a judgmental or critical one.

Despite any "pecking order," acceptance must be given to your boss who gives the nod to a colleague when you wanted the job, the personnel person who passes on your résumé, the driver who cuts you off in traffic, the clerk at Motor Vehicles who is too busy to help, the neighbor who calls the police because of your barking dog, the friend who treats you shabbily, the aunt who spreads gossip in the family, and so forth. You get the point, the list is endless—everyone gets acceptance from you as a member of *Homo sapiens* species. You give it to them as you expect it for yourself.

HOW TO GIVE ACCEPTANCE

- *Think others are adequate.*
- *Treat others as though they are adequate.*
- *Keep giving acceptance even when others seemingly don't deserve it.*

Think others are adequate. Just as you are adequate, others are too. Yes, even that toady, thorn-in-side/pain-in-the-backside lackey, jerk/jerkette, or birdbrain whom you want off your planet. She or he is adequate too and deserves acceptance as a fellow human being.

You are no more important than anyone that you deal with in everyday life. None are less important than you are. Whether they look up to you or not, you can't look down on them. You will never go wrong treating people with more respect than they've ever known before.

You don't have to say out loud to them, "You are adequate." They may mistakenly take it that you're saying, "You are average." You and I know saying "You're adequate" means "You are capable . . . you are up to the task . . . you will prevail."

You do have to think it through. And you definitely can't think or say, "You're inadequate." Now someone's behavior may not be up to par and that needs to be addressed with full-disclosure communication. But as a human, the person is adequate.

When you notice yourself being impatient, autocratic, or snippy with people, stop. Catch yourself. Self-correct. Think a minute how you'd want to be treated if you were on the receiving end.

If you don't give acceptance, you certainly won't get it. If you give it first, you'll be viewed as more impressive yourself. When you give people due respect, they trust you sooner and feel more at ease around you. They are more ready to listen to, discuss something with, and take direction from you.

When someone is on the receiving end of your giving acceptance they will likely appreciate you and want to please. That causes you to support what they are doing even more. You both benefit, and the interchange turns into a "virus" that expands to others. As I heard about New York City Mayor Bloomberg, "His greatest gift is inspiring people to do what they didn't think they could do." Or about Steven Largen, CEO, MacDermid Printing Solutions, "He always makes you do 15 percent better than you thought you could."

Treat others as though they are adequate. This takes energy, I admit. But what you want for yourself, you have to give to others. When you think about them, talk to them, or talk about them to others, choose a neutral or positive perspective. You (1) make their strengths even more significant and their weaknesses sort of irrelevant, (2) let people know they are almost perfect or at least give them the benefit of the doubt, (3) minimize their own fear of rejection.

If you're thinking, "Whoa, that's being overly generous or tender-minded," stop and rethink: That's simply what you want people to do for you. A good start in treating people as adequate is to give them time, interest, and attention. Find something to constructively focus on: quick wit, good with numbers, nice suit, white teeth, new pen, good hair, wonderful integrity, intelligent, kind, on time, or whatever you can bring to mind. Just don't let your mind slip into a "He's not adequate" mode.

Emote "he's adequate" or "she's adequate" followed with "I know you. I know what you can do. I know you can do more than you think you can."

One glamorous talk show host who grew up insecure but turned into a celebrity because of her husband's support and encouragement said, "You will be surprised how quickly you can turn lack of confidence around by saying 'You can. You can. You can.'"

"With the CEO title I have the ability to inhibit or intimidate people. So I try to put people at ease. I smile, I'm open, and I'm the first to say 'hello,'" says Russ Umphenaur, CEO, RTM Restaurant Group. "I want them to know I respect them and don't feel I'm the big cheese."

The least you should do is compliment others. It takes zero effort, no money, and only seconds of your time. It's a good use of some of those 800+ opportunities mentioned in the first chapter. At the least, it's as *Sixty Minutes* curmudgeon Andy Rooney says, "I've learned that just one person saying to me, 'You've made my day!' makes my day."

A good goal is for you to find something or someone to praise today—preferably someone who doesn't expect it or get it a lot from you. The legendary John D. Rockefeller used to hand out dimes. You hand out compliments. It's the simplest and most direct way to treat others as adequate. See people's value, see their worth, and treat them accordingly. Feel it and say it. If you just "feel it," they may never know it, and the opportunity is lost for both of you.

Put down the book, and go find someone and say something you notice. "More than money and sex, people ultimately want recognition and praise," says Lisa Eggerton, public relations executive.

You do a double whammy compliment with something like, "He's so brilliant, he thinks like you do."

Other good compliments:

- "Thank you." (not thanks)

- "That's a good point. I hadn't thought of that."

- "I'm very proud of you."

- "That's a better idea."

- "You're so valued."

- "Do you realize how good of a job you did?"

- "You're just like [fill in the blank with a name of someone important/successful in your sphere]."

When you honestly and sincerely remind people of their special talents, they think you are very wise. Whether they deserve it or not, they generally feel "you're right." Richard Stengel, author of *You're Too Kind,* writes in *Time* magazine, "The higher your self-esteem, the more susceptible to flattery. Confident folks regard the praise directed at them as shrewd judgment rather than sucking up." He goes on to quote Ben Franklin's *Poor Richard's Almanac,* "A flatterer never seems absurd, the flatter'd always takes his word."

My friend Dex has a favorite phrase when he meets laborers on the street, clerks at the grocery store, and other strangers. "You're working too hard," he'll call out. *They* think they are, and it feels good to them to be recognized for it. Even if they really weren't working that hard, the acknowledgment that they exist and aren't invisible feels good.

Dave Hardie, managing director, Herbert Mines Associates, uses appropriate praise this way. "With clients I always find some reason to compliment how they handled the client that I presented. I tell them how good they were at holding up their end of the bargain in the search process. I always find something to compliment and then I'll suggest how, together, we need to handle the next one. With colleagues I simply call them up and say, 'You were fantastic in that meeting. You know more than anyone about [the subject].'"

You can only successfully constructively criticize another's behavior if you've shown you give acceptance to him or her as a person. You can clearly communicate the behavior change you want without implying the person is a bad human being too.

If someone's behavior is unacceptable, address it. Do not attack the person's character, motive, or ability. Stick to the needed behavior change. With an attitude of giving acceptance, you ask questions about what, when, where, why, how the problem started and progressed and how it can be solved. Your facial expression and tone of voice support your attitude and will be discussed in Chapter 4.

ADDRESSING UNACCEPTABLE BEHAVIOR

- "Here's what I want you to do."
- "Here's the resource you have to do it with."
- "Here's the time frame it needs to be done in."
- "Here's what I expect as a conclusion."
- "Any questions?"

All the above is said with thoughts and actions underlined with "you're adequate" to do this. It's not easy, but it is doable.

As one female vice president says, "I try to add value to and bring the best out of others even if it's someone who makes my life a living hell."

Keep giving acceptance even when others seemingly don't deserve it. I know that there are all types of people and some are seemingly more deserving than others, but, who are you and I to judge and categorize? If you were in their hush puppies, you might be doing the very thing that bugs you.

It's surprising how judgmental and critical we can get toward others whom we think are underworking, undermining slough-offs. Then we naïvely think we can keep those thoughts to ourselves! Those thoughts ooze out of every pore of your body when you're around the person and even when you aren't. No one is a good enough actor to camouflage destructive thoughts, at least over time.

Your thoughts maintain and build, or attack and destroy, the esteem of others. You don't have to go overboard with "He is so wonderful; she is so great." You do have to say, "He is adequate, and she is too."

You can never let down your acceptance giving. Five minutes of mismanaged behavior sets you back five months of effectively managed behavior.

Think back to how a harsh word affected you when you were young (or last week)—and how you remember it still. You could be the deliverer of such a negatively remembered message just because you let your guard down. And that momentary letdown can last a lifetime.

To give acceptance is not to forget or dismiss how others think, act, and relate. It still means that you remain vigilantly aware of how others help or harm you. You can be "wisely paranoid" to uncover potential problems so that you can deal with them and still accept those who cause the problem.

Now if someone's character, motive, or behavior is proved harmful and destructive, you must not tolerate it when it affects you and yours. Instead of your first response being to judge and criticize though, it must be to address, clear up, and redirect. If you started out the relationship with straightforward full disclosure, you smoothly continue with this approach when a problem pops up. If you haven't already demonstrated that this is how you deal with problems, then you should start now.

Despite your good intent and effort, some will be suspicious of your giving acceptance. A lot in life is done out of ignorance and innocence, not arrogance. Assuming someone's actions around you stem from a conspiracy to "get you" is wrong. It's just ignorance from lack of experience with you. "Come from a position of goodness" as one executive says. Don't retain obsessive thoughts that people are full of falsehoods, phoniness, hypocrisy, put-ons. They are no more so than you are.

Lynn Canterbury, CEO of Horsetooth Traders says, "I always treat people based on how they deal with me, not based on how others say they treated them."

In truth, people's attitudes and actions around you stem from their own form of self-protection or incompetence or even ignorance. There are enough problems in the world; don't make more problems by not giving people acceptance. Until proven guilty, give others the benefit of the doubt (the same as you'd want). Even after someone is proven guilty, give that person acceptance as a human being while addressing the problem with your full-disclosure communication.

"I'm a judgmental SOB How I'm feeling about others is inversely related to how I feel about myself. I bolster myself by putting others down," are the actual words from one senior executive.

After the open discussion of the problem is satisfactorily completed, initiate a peace-pipe pass. Asking a favor (discussed in Chapter 3) as opposed to doing a favor is a good start.

If someone "does you wrong," Jack Falvey, founder of MakingtheNumbers.com says, one approach is to kill them with kindness. "You may not be able to change things very much, but if you make it a principle to resist taking a most appropriate shot in return and instead attempt to come up with the furthest-out positive thing you can do in reply, you will be able to take great pride in your growth. There can be great humor in dealing with petty tyrants in positive ways."

Just because they don't give acceptance to you is no reason to not give it to them. You can probe, full disclose, and be direct. You have to remember what the six-year-old girl said when the minister asked if she knew what a leader is. "Yes," she said, "It's someone who does the right thing and then people want to follow."

It bears repeating what was said on initiating in Chapter 1: You have to be the first. Besides, lots of times you think people haven't given acceptance to you when really they have but are just not good at showing it. They just aren't good at the "warm and friendly" theatrics of the display. You keep at it regardless of what they do.

By giving acceptance, you might turn them around. But more important, you'll be continuing to hone your skills.

MAINTAIN SELF-ESTEEM

Your number one job in life as a human being is to do all you can to maintain the self-esteem of people around you. People may not remember exactly what you did, how you looked, or what you said, but they will remember how you made them feel.

There is one important thing that you need to do to maintain others' esteem: Give up being totally self-centered. You can't feel like the *Harvard Business Review* cartoon where the husband and wife are leaving church and the husband says, "It was a good sermon, although I didn't like all that stuff about me."

Executive Charisma isn't about you as much as it is about your effect on others. You have a choice to hurt or help their self-esteem. When you improve their self-esteem, they accomplish more, just like you accomplish more when you feel good about yourself. "I feel we have power by words we use to build up or tear down," says Deb Hersh, vice president, Home State Bank. "You can interject a positive thought and it doesn't cost a dime."

Maintaining esteem is to honor and respect—yourself and others. *Self*-esteem breakdown starts with your own attitude management, but it gets fed when others don't give it to you either.

So start by giving it to yourself as well as others. Maintaining someone's self-esteem can start with a little appreciation, a compliment, a favor.

Maury Dobbie, CEO, MediaTech, says, "When I meet someone at my office I always ask 'May I get you a cup of coffee?' It honors them that the CEO will 'fetch' for them, and it honors my administrative assistant because she's got plenty of other work to do."

You do all you can to maintain others' self-esteem. Some won't give it to themselves. You do not have to save them if they want to "drink their own bath water" and "shoot themselves in the foot." You do have an obligation to not chop down whatever esteem and confidence that they do have. Like you, others have a right to have

- Self-satisfaction
- Self-worth
- Self-regard
- Self-respect

On the other hand, too much of a good thing becomes bad. Recent studies at the London School of Economics and Case Western Reserve University have shown that low self-esteem is sometimes not as harmful as very high self-esteem. People with very high self-esteem, for example, were more likely to blast a blaring horn at a stranger in traffic than those with tepid self-esteem. Currently there is a huge controversy in the psychotherapy industry as to whether too much self-esteem is bad for mental health overall. The research showed that people with very high and very low self-esteem impose the biggest threat toward others in a violent way. Those people fill the prisons.

I'm not recommending too high or too low self-esteem; I just want *even* esteem—that being-well-grounded attitude toward self and others—of expecting and giving acceptance as fellow human beings walking this Earth.

Why should you take on what some would say is an unnecessary piece of work? Because it's your job as a human being to do all that you can to maintain others' self-esteem.

**HOW TO MAINTAIN ESTEEM—
YOURS AND OTHERS'**

- *Consistently follow the Golden Rule.*

- *Choose and control your perspective.*

- *Be optimistic, overall, toward yourself, others, and life.*

Consistently follow the Golden Rule. It's pretty basic behavior: What you want for yourself, you give to others. Do right and do it consistently in how you think, act, and relate with people.

Other versions of the "rule" that work:

- Do what's right for the other person, and you'll end up doing what's right for you.

- Do unto others what you would have them do unto you.

- Be good to people, and they will be good to you.

- Treat all people as you would like to be treated.

- Good works on Earth align you in the right way with the universe.

- You never want to do unto others what you would not want done unto you.

- What is hateful to you, do not do to others.

- As a leader, always be more than is expected of the people you're working for and who are working for you.

- You can't ask others to do what you aren't willing to do yourself.

- Treat people like you want to be treated.

- Do unto others before they split.

- How would you want to be treated (or how would you want your mother, your son, to be treated)?

- Treat others as they would like to be treated.

- Don't repeat what you didn't like done to you.

- Expect from others what you expect from yourself.

"I know within five to ten minutes into the interview whether the candidate is right from tangible and concrete evidence. Even if he isn't, I give him the full time. I want him to know he was a valid candidate and worth spending my time with," says one executive recruiter.

No person, no situation, no circumstance should cause you to deviate in your drive to expect and give acceptance to maintain self-esteem. You want it; you do it.

You will lose in your career and in your personal life—despite your substance—if you break down others' esteem. You will never look good by making others look bad, even occasionally.

If you are tired, scared, unprepared, or having a bad hair day, I don't care, stay consistent in this. It's a pretty simple three-step process:

1. Decide to.

2. Stick to it.

3. Repeat 1 and 2.

Don't play to different audiences. There are too many people to try to tailor or adapt to. You're going to forget who gets what. As one person put it, "I try to act the same in a sports bar as I do at the country club." Be the same in front of someone and behind his or her back.

I remember speaking at a five-star hotel for a business group. The person who had hired me was the "queen" of self-esteem building. So pleasant and efficient every time I phoned or emailed. The morning of the presentation I'd done my exercise workout but wanted to check out the location and layout of the room I'd be speaking in later. Dressed in my rather unimpressive sweats and looking, well, "natural" in my hair and makeup, I went to scout out the facility. Since I was hours before the presentation I knew none of my audience would be there and I wouldn't risk being seen. But the meeting planner was there. She didn't recognize me since she'd only seen a photo, and she brusquely brushed past me in the hallway, almost bumping me aside as though she could barely tolerate this less than acceptable individual in her territory. I maintained my anonymity and never spoke of it to her, but I couldn't help but remember it when later in my "dress for success" look she gave me her pleasant side again.

If you don't consistently use the Golden Rule approach, there are people in the world who will suggest that you go where you don't necessarily want to go.

Choose and control your perspective. Your Executive Charisma involves 10 percent of what happens to you and 90 percent of how you react to it. You can seldom choose what goes on in your world but you can always choose your response. It's about choice, *your* choice in choosing the perspective that you want to use.

Now, I'm not suggesting putting a politician's spin (i.e., politesse for lie) to things to make them what they aren't in order to dodge reality. I am suggesting you keep your attitudes in check with an aware, selected, productive, constructive perspective. The right view and the wrong view are always started at the same point, your choice.

Choosing your perspective is as simple as looking at the "other side of the coin." You control your perspective versus letting it be controlled by others. You might even bring a little levity to it like the slogan one kid had on his T-shirt in Breckenridge, Colorado: *Short people have deeper powder.*

Like you, I'm not crazy about email messages that get forwarded to everyone, but the other side of the coin is that sometimes you get one that has some merit. One such message read:

I am thankful:

For the clothes that fit a little too snug, because it means that I have enough to eat.

For all the complaining I hear about the government, because it means that I have freedom of speech.

For the alarm that goes off in the early morning hours, because it means that I am alive.

For the teenager who is not doing dishes but is watching T.V., because that means he is at home and not on the streets.

For the taxes that I pay, because it means that I'm employed.

For a lawn that needs mowing, windows that need cleaning, and gutters that need fixing, because it means I have a home.

For weariness at the end of the day, because it means I have been capable of working hard.

For the parking spot I find at the far end of the parking lot, because it means I am capable of walking and that I have been blessed with transportation.

Well, you get the point.

Whatever happens to you today, turn over the coin. If you have a fender bender, be glad it wasn't worse. If someone is late for an appointment with you, use those extra minutes for yourself. If someone criticizes you, be happy to hear it so you can change and no one will have that to attack in the future. If someone else gets a job that you want, use it as a wakeup call to turn up the juice on your Executive Charisma.

There's something good in everything if you look long and hard enough. So look. Put the effort into choosing your perspective.

When you look at anything, you can choose the attitude, the perspective, that you want to. It's as the poet Maya Angelou writes, "If you don't like something, change it. If you can't change it, change your attitude."

Be optimistic, overall, toward yourself, others, and life. Choose to have a positive outlook underlying everything you do. Just as a food diet depends on what you pick and choose to put in your mouth, in a mental diet you pick and choose what you put into your brain. Stop mental hangovers that give you stomachaches, headaches, extreme fatigue, and bad breath.

Choose your perspective. Better yet, choose a productive, constructive, positive perspective. Don't let anyone rent space in your head with negativism.

Just by thinking one positive thought you're redirecting your moment, your day, your life. Actor Michael Fox talks about how he deals with Parkinson's disease, "I start every day with a good thought, a happy thought, a grateful thought." Your first thought is important but so is your second, third, fourth.

If you tell yourself how bad people, things, and the rest are, you've chosen a negative, destructive approach. What happens is that after about the second, third, or fourth time you replay the thought in your mind, your mind believes it and you end up acting on it. Things get worse than the first time it happened. You create an avalanche out of a snowball.

If you use the mute button on yourself to turn off the self-destructive talk and instead select a positive spin—that just might happen. Then again, it may not happen. But in the meantime you've been using up time and brain cells with the pessimistic gloom and doom.

A friend in Russia told me about her 102-year-old landlady. "Every time she was sick she'd say, 'I'll be better tomorrow,' and she was."

You, of course, must be realistic. I'm the first to want to see things clearly whether it's good or bad news. Always examine the real range of a situation, but don't get prematurely negatively panicky. Few things in life are inherently good or bad, right or wrong. There is almost always another perspective to consider. It's all according to your view.

"God shines on me every day; some days it's cloudy," says Wynn Willard, chief marketing officer, Hershey Foods.

You can have an equally accurate view with a consistent, persistent, constructive, productive, selected perspective.

Martin Seligman, professor of psychology at the University of Pennsylvania, and author of *Learned Optimism: How to Change Your Mind and Your Life* says, "It's the skeleton of hope. . . . If you approach life with a sense of possibility and the expectation of positive results, you're more likely to have a life in which possibilities are realized and results are positive. You'll have a better chance of being promoted, fighting off the cold that's been going around, and attracting people to you—platonically and otherwise. . . . Pessimistic people are two to eight times more at risk of depression . . . [whereas] optimists are less likely to develop cancer or die from heart disease."

"Optimism," writes Lance Morrow in *Time,* "rightly understood, is not a mindlessness but an enabling faculty. Nothing possesses more kinetic energy in a globalizing world."

Optimism is "catching." Moods that start at the top tend to catch on the fastest because everyone watches the boss. They take their emotional cues from him. Even when the boss isn't highly visible—for example, the CEO who works behind closed doors on an upper floor—his attitude affects the moods of his direct reports, and a domino effect ripples throughout the company," writes Daniel Coleman. in *Harvard Business Review.* The leader's mood sets the mood of the people around you. You can create self-defeating negativity, or not.

David Landis, Harvard historian, writes in L. E. Harrison and S. P. Huntington, eds., *Culture Matters: How Values Shape Human Progress* (New York: Basic Books, 2001), "No empowerment is so effective as self-empowerment. In this world, the optimists have it, not because they are always right, but because they are positive. Even when wrong, they are positive, and that is the way of achievement."

Optimism is not a goofy, naïve, over-dreaming perspective. It's choosing to be forward moving regardless of setbacks. It's choosing to be free of unnecessary anxiety, insecurity, and frustration. It's choosing to act void of pessimistic, fuzzy, narrow-minded, overly emotional, nasty, deranged thoughts. No matter how bad things are, accept the fact of where you are, but never let go of the positive mental perspective that "I will prevail."

Yale University conducted a twenty-nine-year study on an optimistic attitude and concluded it was more important to your health than your blood pressure, cholesterol level, smoking, or obesity. You decrease the risk of dying from stroke and cut down your chances of developing heart disease. The study also found that with an optimistic attitude you will live on average seven and one-half years longer.

Optimism is more important than your education, your past, your money, your success. It's certainly more important than your appearance. The remarkable thing is that you have a choice every single day to manage it or let it be mismanaged.

Donald Trump says, "I believe in the power of positive thinking—that you convince yourself to be positive or you convince yourself to be happy. But I don't think you can just say, 'I'm going to be happy, I'm going to be happy, I'm going to be happy.' You have to do things that make you happy."

Fortune reported on the "five steps" leaders need to take charge during a time of crisis. "Embrace brutal optimism" was one of the five.

When in a quandary, choose the optimistic perspective. (Choose it even when not in a quandary.) Seek out what's "positive." When the negative slips in, don't dwell on it in a self-absorbed manner. Instead re-explain the situation with a constructive perspective. The more deep-seated your thoughts are in any mood that you choose, the more deep-seated the thoughts will get—whether negative or positive.

Dave Hardie, managing partner, Herbert Mines Associates, told me about his referencing efforts when recruiting candidates. "It becomes really evident that you should work on establishing relationships, being a leader, dealing with this squishy stuff earlier in your career. Because five years from now someone is going to be calling your boss and asking how you treated people."

3

Ask Questions and Ask Favors

What goes on inside your head is the foundation of your Executive Charisma. With a solid mental foundation you can go out into the world and communicate with people to get things done. It's not sufficient to dispense data and direction alone in your communication. As a leader, you have to get people to execute your ideas in a timely manner. Getting others to execute is most efficiently accomplished by bolstering esteem and also by using the technique of asking questions and asking for favors as a way to ensure your directions are followed willingly.

Asking questions and asking for favors will transfer positive energy from you toward others. You maintain others' esteem while at the same time accomplishing your desired goals. You'll need to be the initiator of the question and favor asking, both up and down the ladder, and inside and outside of your contact circle.

The important thing is not to hold back, not to be afraid, not to feel "it's not your place" to ask. It is. Using the right diplomacy, tone, and manner, you'll find everyone will be receptive to your questions and favor asking!

ASK QUESTIONS

"Ask questions" seems to be very basic advice. Yet it is shocking the number of opportunities you have in a day "to ask" while instead you "tell." To forge a bond as a charismatic executive you'll get better results by asking instead of telling. Asking allows you to learn new information, avoid misinterpretation, solve problems, work your active intelligence, and size up people or situations quickly and accurately. The happiest, most successful people in life ask more than they tell. When you organize your questions, you can be intellectually aggressive without offending. You get respect and attention when you are prepared. You can demonstrate what a good sounding board you are, and showcase your brainstorming ability. You speak up, but not too much. You see how to persuasively deal with a variety of styles and skills. You improve your relationships with other members of the team because they feel valued. People like you better if you ask them things rather than tell them things.

"I learned the importance of asking questions and having good listening skills when I was a little girl. I would sit on a stool at the end of the counter and talk with my Mom while she fixed dinner. I'd spin around and tell her about my day. And she'd say, 'Uh huh, and then what?' I'd talk nonstop about school and when I stopped she'd say, 'Uh huh, and then what?' It was a very valuable lesson in how it felt when someone would actually ask about you and listen to you.

To this day I do the same for others, and it's amazing the things people say to me that they'd never say to others because they know I'll ask and I'll listen," says Kate Hutchinson, senior vice president, marketing, Citrix Systems. She adds, "When you listen you're relating on a different level; you go down more personable avenues. You can develop affinity and trust with each other. It's not just superficial congeniality."

Questions are *not* intended to

- Impress

- Interrogate

- Intimidate

- Dominate

- Embarrass

- Put people in a corner

- "Nail" others on something

- Catch people off guard

- Bust others on something

- Be nosy

- Verbally stalk

Questions *are* intended to

- Give acceptance

- Maintain esteem

- Focus on others instead of yourself

- Delegate better

- Learn

- Verify what you already know

- Test what you think

- Handle surprise and attack

- Provide small talk

When you ask, you learn. Most of us know a lot less than we think we do. You may find out something you didn't know or confirm something you already knew. You learn what people actually care about. You foster a learning spirit for what's going on in the world.

Questions help you confirm or verify what you know or think you know. Ask instead of assuming. Ask when you already know the answer. Ask, "Where are we in agreement, where are we in disagreement?" or a simple, "Have I made myself clear enough?"

If something can be interpreted in more than one way, it will be, and usually not the way you wanted. With questions you can be direct and to the point. You avoid mutual mystification, hinting, innuendo, and wild guesses where neither party knows what's really being said or going on. "Don't expect, inspect," is how one CEO put it to me. Leave absolutely nothing to chance by asking.

An advertising agency had lost a client. The representative said to me, "We were perplexed as to what to do. So I went back in and asked, 'What would it take to get you back?' and he told me. I just had to ask. It was simple, brilliant common sense."

It's important *how* you ask in choice of words and tone of voice. For instance, you suspect something "questionable" is going on. You could blurt out, "You're lying to me." Or, you could simply ask, "Do you know for a fact that's the truth?" With the first approach, whether the person is being honest or not, he or she will be defensive and that won't get you closer to the truth. The second approach lets the individual maintain self-esteem by explaining what's going on, or it lets the person dig him- or herself deeper into a hole if he or she is lying.

With questions you delegate, manage, and lead more effectively. If you direct without asking for input, you're dictating and forcing people to "just follow orders." You won't effectively get things done through people in that manner. If instead you ask for input in a directed sense to get people to come up with a solution "on their own," you maintain their self-esteem. With an organized "brainstorm" they avoid guessing and ending up wrong. As the leader, you likely already know or want a specific solution. Your directed questions help them come up with the solution you want. When they come up with the good answer, based on the wise questions you ask to ensure they come up with the good answer, everyone wins. It's up to you to ask questions—the *right* questions—to get them to the right answers.

Sometimes it is necessary to say, "Do it 'cause I told you to." Just remember to use questions before, during, and after such directness, and your instructions will be more favorably received and you'll get better follow-through.

Questions help you handle surprise and attack better. "What do you mean?" works whenever you're caught off guard. "What's that based on? Can you give me an example? Why do you think that?" all would be better than a defensive position on your part.

Questions are good for casual (and serious) conversations with people. "I hate small talk," is a complaint I often hear. Small talk doesn't have to be chitchat about nonsense. Good small talk is good question asking. "When, what, where, how, why" works anytime and anywhere. Think back to the Golden Rule and ask yourself, "What would I like to be asked or told about?" and start there. Avoid what you wouldn't want to be asked or told.

Mark Gunn told me about a meeting with Colin Powell. "He has a great ability for dialogue. In the first fifteen minutes of our meeting he did nothing but ask questions. He'd ask about something five different ways to get an arm around his own point of view. He'd ask clarifying questions, 'I heard you say. . . . I've had an experience, are there any similarities?' Questions on questions that he'd already asked. Powell understands because of his position he has to ask first before he gives his opinion. If he puts out his opinion too fast, people will want to jump on his side and form theirs likewise. He wants you to give yours first. He's a master of dialogue."

HOW TO ASK QUESTIONS

- *Choose your words and tone carefully.*
- *Keep your questions organized.*
- *Volunteer information without being asked.*

Choose your words and tone carefully. You have to be careful choosing how and what you ask. "What do you mean?" when said in a sincere inquisitive tone is effective. The same question spoken in a threatening tone becomes an ineffective accusation, "What do you mean by *that*!"

The flight attendant who asks, "Is your seat all the way up, Sir?" is more effective than the one barking out, "Put your seat up, *okay Sir*?"

When you ask a question, be direct and courteous. Don't let your voice sound emotional or your expression look like you've got a hidden agenda. The same tone of voice that you'd use when you say, "Please pass the salt" is best. Choose questions that you'd be receptive to if asked of you. (It's that Golden Rule thing again.)

Don't speak off the cuff or wing it. You can plan and still have spontaneity in your querying. Write down good questions that you've heard or ones asked of you, and then commit them to memory or paper to ask someone else. When I talked with Doug Conant, CEO of Campbell Soup, to gain from his experience and to get his opinion on what I'm writing, his first words to me were, "How can I help you?" Later in the conversation I mentioned the positive effect that question had. He said a longtime mentor of his always asked that when he answered his phone. Conant liked it, and continues to use it himself.

Maybe some of these questions will inspire you, and you can incorporate them in your own communication style:

- What was your proudest accomplishment last year?

- What is the biggest accomplishment you're working on this year . . . this month . . . in your life?

- What was the smartest decision you made . . . this month . . . in your life?

- What was the kindest, most generous-spirited thing you saw someone else do?

- What are you happiest about completing (or starting) this year?

- Who was the person (or people) who had the greatest impact on your life last year . . . ever?

- What was the biggest risk you took recently . . . or in your life?

- What compliment were you proudest to receive?

- What advice do you constantly give yourself?

- What are you most committed to changing or improving in your life . . . your work . . . yourself?

- What would make you most happy to do this year?

- Have you been anywhere recently that you enjoyed?

- What can I do to brighten your day?

Here are some questions to avoid (to name a few!):

- Had any surgery lately?

- Ever been in prison?

- What's your religious, political, or sexual inclination?

Keep your questions organized. Consider your objective: to learn, verify, confirm, persuade, delegate, confront, reject, and so on. Then select questions that aid in meeting your objective. "Asking good, tough questions generates respect from a leader," says Paul Schlossberg, president, DFW Consulting.

If you don't pre-think, organize, and rehearse your questions, you'll miss your target. If you think out your questions and keep them organized, you'll get done what you need to get done, faster and more effectively. Others will value you more when you value their time by your organized approach to getting things done. And when you get a reputation for asking good questions, people feel they owe it to you to answer with better preparation.

Don't make questions tricky or complicated: Simple, direct, relative, and clear works best. "Would you explain?" Why, how, when, and what questions work well. Don't try to be clever with your questions. Clever questions can backfire.

Simple doesn't mean mundane. "How are you? What do you do? Where are you from?" need more interesting phrasing. "You look good, how are you?" "I've seen you around, what do you do at . . .?" "I'm from Colorado, where do you hail from?"

If you just have one "issue" to question, ask about it three times in three slightly different ways to get past the glib answer. For example, you might ask first, "How would you describe your leadership style?" Let them answer. Then ask, "Can you give me an example that has worked very well?" Let them answer. Then ask, "What areas are you working on to change and improve on your style?" Typically you have to ask about the same issue more than once because people are too lazy to answer fully, too skeptical to initially open up, too unprepared to give the complete and accurate answer on the first pass. Plus you make the exchange more conversational and less interrogatory.

A good rule of thumb is that for every five minutes of conversation, you should ask five questions. "Who, what, why, when, and how" about business, food, or trips covers your five questions. Starting with small questions that lead to bigger questions is a good way to organize your question asking.

Keeping the end in mind is also a good organizational tool. Jack Falvey, founder, MakingtheNumbers.com, recommends that salespeople ask testing-the-waters questions: "Can you agree to that?" "Should this be the next step?" "If that's so, can we do this?" Which should lead to "Can we do business together?"

Anything you need to communicate can best be done with questions. To practice, try a day of framing everything that needs to be done in a question format. Absolutely everything you say, think, or give an opinion on, you do with a question. (It can actually be practiced as a party game, where you're "out" of the game when you make a statement instead of asking a question.)

Compare the outcome of question-based conversation against a day of telling-based ones. You'll find you get more accomplished, more effectively, with less effort in the question day.

The more you ask the more you'll know. The more you know the more you'll understand. The more you understand the more you'll care. The more you care the more they'll care about you and yours.

Volunteer information without being asked. In addition to asking questions, you must also judiciously volunteer information to keep balance in the conversation. If you only ask and "take" but not "give," people will stop answering.

People who want to answer what you asked don't want to feel interrogated or put on the spot when you ask. So, as you ask, self-disclose too. It has to be a two-way street, not one-way for either of you. When and how you volunteer (or don't volunteer) sets the tone for others to respond to. You'll get what you give.

Be the first to volunteer information about yourself as you ask about others. Volunteering information without waiting to be asked shows self-confidence. You simultaneously show that you expect acceptance and give it as you "take people into your confidence." Scared people hide and withhold information; confident ones don't. "I give a little and then I always get more back," says Michele Fitzhenry, vice president, TRRG.

HOW TO ANSWER QUESTIONS

Be as willing to respond to questions as you are willing to ask them. If you hesitate to answer, people think you aren't cooperative, don't know the answer, don't know what you're doing, or that you lack confidence. You might even be viewed as acting arrogant and superior in your nonresponse.

Choose your words and tone carefully to hit the right degree of clarity. Listen to what the question is. Keep a "pass the salt" tone of voice with no hidden agenda emotion. Maintain a relaxed facial expression (more about that in Chapter 4).

Attentively lean forward to answer the questions simply, concisely, truthfully, and targeted to the audience. Follow the *USA Today*'s slogan: "Not the most words, just the right ones." Keep the answers organized. Use complete sentences. End sentences. Provide one thought at a time.

Practice important or complicated answers when you're not on the hot seat so that the answers come to you more readily when you are. Think about what you should, could, or want to answer to a question. Rehearse it in your head, and depending on the importance, rehearse it on a tape recorder. (If you don't have a tape recorder you can call your own voice mail and tape it on there for playback.) Listen and think how it will sound to others and how they'll likely react. Change your wording if necessary to get the reaction you want.

continued

Try out different words to test the different effects. Follow the instruction given to airline pilots who are taught to select words that minimize travelers' anxiety. The phrasing "The new departure or arrival time is . . ." is better than the word "late." The word "gate" is preferable to "terminal." And "destination" sure beats "final destination."

Choose descriptive words since they have their own body language: For example, "We get a lot of referrals" is bland compared to, "We get a beautiful number of referrals." "We work well together," is less convincing than "We work in harmony."

If you don't know the answer, say you don't and then go find it out. Don't fake or try to fool with the hope that "if you throw things against the wall some will stick." Don't attempt to show how much you know when in truth you're disorganized and nervous and don't know. "I don't know but I'll find out," works.

"Yes" and "no" are perfectly acceptable answers to almost every question. They avoid the groan, "How short the question; how long the answer."

"That's something I choose not to answer," can be your response if they are just being nosy. You don't have to answer every question (just as they don't have to answer yours), but it does tend to stop the conversation flow.

"I'm just going to skip that question" is an answer that works sometimes. It's more straightforward than what politi-

continued

cians are taught in the art of "nonanswer." As former White House insider George Stephanopoulos explains it, "The fundamental rule is to shoehorn what you want to say into the answer no matter what the question is."

If you keep getting the same questions, you're not answering well. Answer, and then ask, "Is that what you were asking?" or "Does that answer the question?" to make sure you did. Keep it a conversation, not an interview. Pay attention to micro-questions the person is asking. Pay attention to people's answers to your questions. You need to hear and know their interests and priorities to determine the answers you need to give and questions you need to continue to ask.

Return to questions that were unanswered by you because they got skipped over with "Something I may not have explained well. . . ." It shows you listen, remember, and take responsibility to answer as asked.

ASK FAVORS

Just as you need to ask questions, you need to ask favors. You might mistakenly think that if you "do" for others, others will appreciate and value you. They might, but they also might end up resenting you because your favor has caused them to "owe" you in return.

Therefore, you have to *ask* favors first. You ask not so much to "get" something but rather to "give" others an opportunity to help. You save them from owing you. You hand power to them in a disarmingly open way. People like that. They feel valued.

"It's a way of paying a compliment and puts people in a position where they are more comfortable. I go way out of my way to ask favors," says John Krebbs, CEO, PAC.

If you do a favor first, those people feel indebted to you. "Giving" obligates. People don't want to "owe." They don't like that. It is more empowering to be "asked of" than "done for."

If a favor is done for you, causing you to now owe someone, you can "pay back" with a favor. The favor you were likely going to do anyway. But because of your forethought and consideration, you keep balance in the relationship. You've initiated the give and take that is necessary in any effective relationship.

If you wait for give and take it might end up with give and give. You are not valued when you do that. You are used. There is actually a term I've heard coined for such extreme favor doers: Generous Idiot. Remember, what I've repeatedly said: Anything good taken to the extreme becomes bad.

Please don't take my advice to the extreme and cease doing favors. Just cease only doing favors and not asking favors too.

One CEO told me, "Well, I never want to owe anyone." Just like you don't want to "owe," others don't either. So when you ask, they respond, and you respond—no one owes anybody and the relationship maintains its integrity.

You aren't asking them to do something as much as you are giving them the opportunity to help you. You initiate the back and forth. You foster rapport by asking, not by obligating them.

"I practice every day to ask a favor. It makes people feel valued and I learn. I was considering starting my own practice so I asked a client if I could take him into my confidence. He said he'd love the opportunity to share his opinion, even adding he'd like to be on my advisory board. I used to spend hours giving myself reasons not to ask. I don't do that anymore because the results are so fantastic with such little effort," says a lawyer friend of mine.

Asking favors to bond isn't a new concept. Ben Franklin wrote, "If you want to make a friend, let someone do you a favor." Churchill talked to his lieutenants about an enemy of Churchill's, saying he didn't know why the individual disliked him so much. He hadn't done him a favor. The Greek philosopher, Plutarch, wrote around 100 A.D. "We like people for whom we do favors more than people who do favors for us."

When you ask favors first, you

- Allow others to be and feel useful

- Drive reciprocity

- Save doing it all

You can actually strip people of self-respect when you do for them as if they can't do for themselves. Doing for others first does not get followers; asking first does.

Some people purposely use doing favors to make people indebted. "Building my pile of chits" as one executive put it. Lots of time, doing favors isn't so much helping people but a show of your own power. It's a reverse hook they put in you.

If you "do" first and they don't give back, don't feel resentful for their not returning the favor. Remember:

- It was your choice to do the favor.

- No one owes you anything; no victims here.

- You can choose to do more in hopes they'll do something.

- You can choose to cease doing.

- You can ask them for a favor.

"I usually do more favors than I ask so that when I need a favor there is no hesitation for folks to do it. I will usually ask for favors if there is no other good way to get something done. Sometimes I will ask 'favors' not so much to get something done but rather to engage someone in the goals I am trying to achieve and have them feel some identification, ownership, and commitment to the goals," says Gene Pope, vice president, e-commerce platforms, Amazon.

Whatever you choose, give acceptance and maintain self-esteem.

It's conceivable that they didn't notice your favor, didn't think it was one, didn't think it was a good one, didn't want it done, or consciously or unconsciously chose to ignore it.

"Ask for favors regularly. The relationships you develop as a result of asking favors are immeasurable. Be tactful and charming. Do not be a pest, and sense if you are going too far. By asking for favors you open yourself for the return of favors. Be the first to volunteer and show you are willing to 'help.' Give, give, and give some more. This does not have to mean money; it could be just assisting with a little thing and enjoying the pleasure of giving of yourself. Do your favor willingly, genuinely, and quickly. If you are not in a position to assist when a favor is asked, say you will try to find a person who can help but do not promise and then not do it," says Ted Wright, CEO, The Aslan Group.

Asking a question is a small favor. You're asking for information, help, confirmation, and so on. People feel valued when you ask of them. You maintain their esteem. A simple, "Tell me if you can . . ." will get an "of course I can!"

Asking for favors is not to make someone go out of their way or to impose or to be impertinent. Favors aren't for the purpose of getting out of doing something you should be doing yourself.

When you do for others, most people want to respond or retain balance in the relationship. But some people feel no obligation. They even make it clear, verbally or nonverbally, that they won't be obligated to return your favor. That's their choice. If they aren't willing to "play ball" you want to know early on. Better find that out so you can choose how to act with them.

It bears repeating that you should not resent a refusal. Remember, you're not owed even if you have done favors first. Doing something for someone else was your choice. One executive told me, "I will do favors for quite a while until I see the balance tipped dramatically. It would be nice of them to return it. If they don't, I'll stop. It speaks to their lack of awareness if they don't reciprocate."

"It's not my nature to ask, but relationships have gotten stronger when I do. People want to do things for you and I accept that," says one marketing manager.

HOW TO ASK FOR FAVORS
- *Ask: Would you do me a favor?*
- *Keep it simple. Be specific.*
- *Thank them.*

Ask: Would you do me a favor? Soon to be followed with, "I owe you. How can I help you?" Ask for something you really do need. Choose something that is doable. If you set them up with something impossible or improbable you set them up for failure. Your tone of voice and manner shouldn't be pleading or needy. Pass-the-salt works well.

Don't offer a compliment at the same time you ask a favor. People will be wary of you. It's like charging for the praise. "Would you do me a favor?" and "Thanks so much," is good. Thank the person later, again. If possible tell someone else about the favor, thus doubling the thank you.

Be direct, don't be cagey. Tell them what you want and when you want it. If the deadline is coming up, remind them so they don't disappoint themselves (and you). "A man called me last week who I had met two years ago. He said he finally got the nerve to remind me of a favor he'd asked. I immediately called him and did what I could. He was floored," says Jerome Davis, president, Americas, EDS Business Process Management.

Barbara Hamer, Georgetown University, offers the letter shown below as a good example of asking a favor and interestingly enough doing a favor simultaneously. (Incidentally, the book referred to in the letter is my book, which Barbara Hamer had requested permission to quote from earlier, thus asking me for a favor too—one that I didn't mind doing, of course.)

Barbara asked a doable favor in a straightforward manner. By making this request, she also makes Jane Doe feel important and powerful. Jane will undoubtedly try to do something to reinforce this implied power to act on someone's behalf. Moreover, it causes her to think highly of Barbara and her good judgment. Jane will feel more comfortable asking Barbara for some help in something in the future. Sally Smith might get a job from it and will be eager to return the favor for both Barbara and Jane. You can see that the ramifications of a small positive gesture just go on and on and on.

Dear Jane,

Here's hoping that you are well and enjoying life. I am well and my position here at Georgetown continues.

Enclosed is the résumé of a good friend of mine. Her name is Sally Smith. She is job hunting. In one of our conversations, she mentioned her interest in the XYZ organization. And I thought, "Bingo, I know Jane Doe."

All I can do is send you Sally's résumé. I feel strongly in women networking with other women. It was how I got my position here. If you can think of a director, manager, or chief with whom Sally might interview, I'm sure she would be appreciative.

I read in *How to Think Like a CEO* a few years ago that "I'm not fearless but I will take risks." Whenever anyone decides to help someone, it is always a risk and yet, if one does not stick his/her neck out once in awhile, what is ever gained? XYZ may not have a position at this moment for Sally. On the other hand, she may be the greatest thing that ever walked into your life.

Thank you for reading my letter. I'll keep my fingers crossed that Sally will hear from you.

Sincerely yours,

Barbara Hamer

Keep it simple. Be specific. "I really need your help in . . . . I'd like your opinion on . . . . I'm kind of having a problem with . . . . It would be wonderful for me if . . . . Could you ask Mary to set up an appointment with . . . . Would you suggest whom I talk with on . . . ?"

Tell people what or when or how or why you need something. Make it easy for them to do the favor. It saves them time, effort, and guessing. Be helpful not bossy, of course.

I had a CEO client ask me to introduce him to an author I know. Coincidently, at about the same time, that very author asked me to introduce him to the very same CEO!

They both told me what they wanted by when. I phoned their administrative assistants, asked if they'd do me a favor by telling me their respective bosses' favorite restaurants. When the same one came up for both, I asked the administrative assistants to schedule a dinner for them together. The two ended up doing a business deal together.

Neither one ever forgot the favor I did for them. The irony is that they did me the favor by asking me to do the favor so I could in fact do them a favor.

Don't overdo it. Know how much is too much to ask. It's too much if you set them up to fail, disappoint, or show their lack of power. It's too much if it's a major effort or anything you just don't want to do and you guess they don't want to do either. They will resent you more than if you had done them a big favor originally.

A good favor is asking someone for career-related advice. That's all networking is: asking mentors and role models for their opinions on jobs, careers, companies. That's a perfect favor. You show that you value their experience by asking for some of it. It's painless to provide, they feel important, you learn, and you can give back to them sometime in the future out of appreciation. When they give advice, listen.

Do not use or take advantage of others, but do not hesitate to ask for fear of imposing. If your favor is unreasonable, they won't do it anyway.

Thank them. Thank them for doing the favor, just short of profusely. Tell someone else about the favor, if it makes the giver look good, *not* you the recipient. They probably won't immediately ask for a return favor, but you should immediately do something anyway to keep the balance in your mind and theirs. Clip an article of interest about their company or their competition, send a book, mail company samples, and so on.

"A highly coveted trait in business relationships is that of being grateful," says Michael Nieset, partner, Heidrick & Struggles. "Be grateful and show that you are. A question like 'Would you do me a favor . . . I'd be grateful,' and later, 'Thank you,' works well."

When *you* are asked a favor, do it genuinely and quickly. Be flattered; don't be leery or hesitant or suspicious. Be receptive.

Do what they ask if you can, or do what you can, within your means to do what was asked. Evaluate the desirability of the favor and your willingness and ability to do it. If it isn't a wise thing to do, give an alternative.

Provide a contact or a connection to help them move faster to a successful result. A friend and his daughters met Britney Spears on the street in New York City. The girls asked to have a picture taken. Spears's bodyguard stepped up and said, "No photos allowed. But if you give me your mailing address we will have an autographed copy of Ms Spears sent to you." She offered an alternative that fit what she was willing to do.

"I feel flattered, and nine out of ten times I want to be helpful. The tenth time is usually someone stepping too far which actually creates a barrier," says one engineer.

John Krebbs, CEO, PAC, says, "I go way out of my way to help when asked. If I've been used, so what. It's just intellectual property. There's no shortage."

After you do a favor don't say or imply, "I did one for you, now you owe me" and don't silently feel owed. Don't keep score.

Create an opportunity to ask one back if they want and if they don't, so what.

"I remember something my roommate in college used to do. He'd offer me some candy with 'please, take some.' His words and attitude suggested that it would be an honor for him to have his candy taken. Then I didn't feel like I was sponging off him," says Bob Berkowitz, host of *Naked New York,* talking about favors. "I also recall a time when I was in China on assignment for ABC. I met some man who was going to take me to his house for dinner. Since he hadn't the opportunity to notify his wife I asked if we could stop and buy her some flowers because I was going unannounced. He said, 'No, in China we give you the gift for coming to our house because you honor us by coming into our home.'"

It takes some thought to figure out the back and forth of favors. But, do yourself a favor, and think about it; then try today.

4

Stand Tall, Straight, and Smile

You are always being watched by someone when you're out in public, that's why they call it the "public eye." You might hope that people won't always notice you but they do notice. In the public eye you have no "stunt double" and there is no "instant replay" for your behavior. How you act shapes people's opinion of you. The scrutiny is a little nerve wracking, but it's as they say in the song, "If you're going to make a livin', you got to put on a good show."

Don't say, "Well, I don't care what people think about how I look." You're fooling yourself. You do care or you wouldn't wear clothes and live in a house and work for a living. You don't *care* so much that you compromise yourself, of course. But you should care to the degree that you give them what you want them to see when they *are* looking.

At work you might think that you get a "personnel review" once a year at your company. Wrong. You get reviewed every day. It's an informal, unspoken review that you get in the company lunchroom, parking garage, hallways, and in every business and social meeting. It's wherever, whenever, forever. Being watched is how "hi-pots" (high potential people) are identified. It's the way lo-pots are identified as well!

I once noticed a company president reading the name tags remaining on the registration desk after a meeting had started. I then heard him query the registrar if everyone in attendance had taken a name tag. She told him yes. After he walked into the meeting room, the registrar said to me, "These 'name tag' leavers won't be with the company next year if he has anything to do with it." Even when you aren't there, you're being watched.

One executive told me that he takes notes at meetings on what his people say and how they say it. Later he speaks to each person in private about his observations. Whether you like being watched and judged or not, it happens. You must do what you can to have people see what you want them to see instead of leaving it to misinterpretation. It's a challenge, but it's also an opportunity. This is required in all walks of life. The founder of the rock group Phish, Trey Anastasio, says, "There's a lot more to being a rock star than music. You have to act like an idiot publicly . . . and you have to go to award shows."

Most of the time you go about your business without the conscious awareness of being watched. But there are times when you definitely should be aware of it. Some people saw an obvious example when Senator Hillary Clinton sat in the televised audience as President Bush addressed the nation after September 11. Dominick Dunne wrote about it in *Vanity Fair,* "I have stuck by Hillary Clinton through thick and thin. . . . But she lost me on September 20 with her appalling manners during President Bush's magnificent speech to Congress and the nation. What was her problem? She looked mad and mean, with a scowl on her face and a hard glint in her eye. . . . How strange, I thought, the second time the camera cut to her, that a person who had lived in the public eye as the First Lady for eight years could allow herself to be caught in that mood."

Most of us will never be analyzed by the nation's public eye, but in our own smaller world we're watched just as much. Don't let the fact that you're *being inspected* bother you or feel *victimized* by the fact that you are constantly observed. It happens to everyone. It's called "people watching." Ted Wright was the managing director of an Australian hotel, The Regent. Any "bigwig" going to Sydney was his guest. The people in his circle of contacts included Luciano Pavarotti, Margaret Thatcher, King Juan Carlos, Tom Brokaw, Donald Trump, Robert Redford, Barbara Walters, Ralph Lauren, just to name a few. Wright, himself, was even knighted by the Queen. (This is quite a background for a University of Nebraska graduate.) He says, "The ones who have 'it' seem to have a certain state of mind when they walk into a room. Generally they are well-groomed, calm, self-assured, and have control of themselves. They have great eye contact, but their twinkling eyes are also moving as they size up a room. The impressive ones are affable, friendly, polite, and very interested in the other person. One man was particularly good at walking up to you and making you feel like you were the only guy in the room as he asked you questions and allowed you to ask him questions. He kept his answers short. The tone of voice was correct. When you saw him later he remembered your name. He delivered a perception of confidence and I had to also. . . . Now, not all were that way. Some did seem to have a charisma bypass despite the money they made."

Your Executive Charisma requires theatrics. In my book, *How to Think Like a CEO,* I wrote about the twenty-two vital traits required to be the person at the top. One was "being a tad theatrical." Theatrical is not artifice. It is being aware of and responsible for the effect you have on people around you through your physical presence.

Anyone who tells you this isn't important is fooling him- or herself and worse, trying to fool you. You and everyone else "acts" all of the time—some good, some bad, some prepared, some not.

An actor friend told me, "We all get the same script. Acting ability and how you treat the script is what gets you the job." Even in business, we all pretty much get the same script, that being the same problems, frustrations, opportunities, missed opportunities, politics, power plays, and the rest. Standing tall, straight, and smiling will make the difference between success and lack of success in your physical approach to these problems.

Five minutes of the right "theatrics" can be worth five *months* or even five years of hard work. The downside is that five minutes of the wrong stuff (being "impaled on a single mistake" as one CEO put it) takes you five months or maybe five years to dig out from under. During the Olympics, I heard a commentator for the ice skaters say, "One little mistake during a four-minute program cancels out four years of training." (Don't be frustrated if you're now thinking of the times you messed up. You can take heart in the fact that people are so starved for good leaders that they will forgive a lot of missteps in the past if you finally get it right now.)

One executive said, "My style at meetings is to remain totally impassive while I twirl a pencil between the thumb and index finger of each hand. Even if I have nothing to say at the meeting, it makes me appear to be a silent, judgmental presence. And when I'm ready to say something, I wait for a pause in the whining drone and break a pencil angrily. It always gets everyone's attention." I neither recommend nor condemn his choice of theatrics. I do promote the fact that he has thought about the effect he wants to have and takes action to generate the effect. He has planned his five seconds of spontaneity.

Think how you want to be seen a year from now (or two or ten years). If you start there and work back it's much easier to see what you need to do today toward that goal. Hugh Hefner did that in the 1960s when he created a picture of the perfectly balanced man whom he called "Mr. Playboy."

Rolling Stone magazine writes, "[Hefner] knew that he was no Mr. Playboy. He didn't dress well, he didn't socialize well, and he didn't live a very exotic life. It was time to make some changes, he decided. Fast changes.

"So in December 1959, Hugh Hefner began his metamorphosis. First, he took out a massive bank loan and purchased a multistory, red brick and limestone palace on Chicago's Gold Coast. Next, he put $1 million into renovations, building an indoor pool, a movie theater, and, the pièce de résistance, an underwater bar, where guests could sip drinks while watching Playmates swim naked. He parked a convertible white Mercedes Benz in front of the house, along with a Mercedes limousine, complete with two orange flags bearing the rabbit head logo, and for his personal image, he purchased a red-velvet smoking jacket, which he thought would appear especially sophisticated if it were worn while smoking a hand-carved pipe, so he bought one of those, too."

Please know I'm not suggesting you model yourself after Hefner, but the deliberate, self-aware, disciplined, thorough approach he took is worth some consideration. You could criticize such a "constructed persona" but don't. Who doesn't similarly self-invent? Politicians, celebrities, yes even CEOs put themselves together for their own impersonation of the "person" they want to be. When preparing for President Clinton's first inauguration address, at the last minute it was discovered that he didn't know how to salute, since he hadn't been in the military. He quickly had to learn how to do it to complete the symbolism of taking office.

There's a lot that figures into the picture when you construct your physical style—dress, hair, gestures, props, "attitude"—but regardless of the extent to which you take it, the least and the most important is to stand tall, straight, and smile.

CLOTHES AND EXECUTIVE CHARISMA

As they say, clothes don't make the man but they do make a difference. Of course, there is the argument that clothes do make the man because naked people have little influence in our society.

Quite frankly, clothes are the least important part of your physical presence, but they are part. Fortunately, they are the easiest to do something about.

A basic objective when you view clothes is to "wear your performance." That's why people dress extra spiffy for job interviews. If you do well, you should look like you do.

continued

Business, as all of life, is based on perception. If you look like a leader in your dress and demeanor even before you are, people will perceive you as such sooner.

The acceptance of business casual dress does not mean it's acceptable to be *casual* in comportment.

"Leaders reflect a confidence and it shows in their faces, the way they walk and the way they dress. They usually understand the 'costume thing.' To say all leaders are great dressers would be incorrect, but they do look like they are naturally fitted into the gear they are wearing for whatever and wherever the event or forum. They can be tall or short, slim or round, yet they are 95 percent of the time in tune with the 'what' that they are communicating by what they wear and how they wear it. Look at Churchill, George Patton, Condoleezza Rice, John F. Kennedy, Fidel Castro, Douglas MacArthur, Saddam Hussein, Arafat, and Bill Clinton. Leaders look like they are in charge, as a rule. If you care about the little things such as what you wear, you probably care about a lot of other little and big things as well. A leader usually looks imposing. Even Gandhi in his special way commanded the attention by the way he dressed," says Ted Wright, CEO, The Aslan Group.

To make the clothes issue simpler:

Select a dominant color: black, navy, tan, gray, brown, and buy the best quality and style (which doesn't mean trendiest style) that you can in that color in every piece of

continued

clothing and accessory. (One CEO said he didn't choose "black" he chose "gunfighter black.") You get your wardrobe pulled together quicker and can travel easier with one color. Consistency in dress implies consistency in behavior. You can keep one color from being boring with your selection of ties, or shirts, jewelry, scarves, and so on.

Rotate the old out. Just as you adopt new business trends, adopt (within reason) fashion changes. (For example, if ties/lapels are narrow, go with narrow; don't stay with wide.) You don't have to be on the cutting edge, but you don't want to look dated either. One CEO I know buys a new pair of shoes and immediately gives away an old pair. He does the same with shirts, jackets, slacks, and so on. Nothing new goes into his closet without something old coming out.

Unless everything fits perfectly, regularly alter clothes to fit you. If you gain or lose weight, it's cheaper than a new wardrobe—and it's a necessity for your appearance.

You should dress the way you want those around you to dress, since subordinates will tend to emulate the leader's attire. Then turn it up a notch, making your dress just a hair better to meet the image people have of a leader.

When attending a special event, research the expected dress in advance. Find out what's typical, and choose your attire accordingly. Dressy clothes aren't just for special occasions but to make an occasion special. Even if you are sim-

continued

ply presenting a plaque at lunch with three colleagues, your attire should still befit the accomplishment.

If casual is the norm at your office, keep a "dress up" outfit stored there for emergency situations. Have a complete "might need" outfit set aside and marked for your administrative assistant or significant other to ship overnight to any location when needed.

A final word on clothes: It's more important *how* you wear them than *what* you wear. Standing tall and straight makes any type of clothes look better because they hang better on your body.

Despite my emphasis on being aware of your *own* attire, don't be judgmental toward others. Don't give the suited person preference, respect, or attention over the casually dressed person. Both get the same treatment as in everything in this book. Besides, you never know who has the most influence in what you're trying to do.

STAND TALL AND STRAIGHT

People may measure your ability according to what *they see* more than what you say or do. You have to ensure that the message you send is the message you intend. There are physical behavior patterns expected in leaders that entail posture, demeanor, comportment, and overall appearance.

Ambassador Madeleine K. Albright delivered the commencement address at Wellesley College speaking about Cold War history,

UN peacekeeping, nuclear arms, restoring democracy to Haiti, and the universal status of women. Then she ended the speech with "So congratulations, good luck, and remember always to sit up straight."

Why in the world would she end such an important speech with such seemingly insignificant advice about posture?

Stand tall and straight summons up visions of someone ethical, courageous, awake, alert, and alive. Good posture shows confidence, vitality, discipline, and youthfulness. Slumped posture implies fright, insecurity, lack of self-acceptance or self-control, lack of discipline, a loser, sheepishness, shame, and guilt. To stand tall and straight is to have a demeanor that says, "I expect acceptance."

Your outward behavior should be congruent with your inward attitude. Even if it isn't, people think it is. They "read" you and make conclusions based on what they see.

When you walk into a meeting, have a spring in your step and a smile on your face and say with enthusiasm, "Let's get started." The others will look at you and respond, "Yes, let's." In seconds you will have transformed them by your words and appearance. And you just might encourage them to walk right in and look confident with their people who are going to make things happen. If you want to be a great "player," you have to walk, look, and act like a great player.

On the other hand, if you schlep in, hunched over, physically crumbled, and say, "Let's get started." They'll think, "Yeah, let's get started by replacing you!"

When you enter a room it's yours, or it isn't, depending on your physical presence.

Your comportment causes people to conclude something about you. We describe character with expressions about physical appearance: can't look you in the eye . . . head's on backward . . . clams up . . . tight-lipped . . . speaks out of the side of his mouth . . . rises to the occasion . . . level-headed . . . eagle-eye . . . wide-eyed . . . stands on her own two feet . . . tongue-tied . . . glad-hands . . . hand-wringing . . . wandering eye . . . squares his shoulders . . . snaps out of it . . . slappin' on the back . . . weak-kneed . . . backbone . . . steady eye . . . takes others at face value . . . you can see the quit in his eye . . . and, of course, *stands tall and straight.*

In *Newsweek,* Barbara Franklin, a corporate board of director says, "Directors are sitting straighter in their chairs. There's a lot more vigilance."

An interesting and ironic quote from Helen Keller, considering her blindness, was, "Never bend your head. Hold it high. Look the world straight in the eye."

HOW TO STAND TALL AND STRAIGHT

- *Do with what you have.*
- *Lift up, suck in, and breathe.*
- *Decide to live the rest of your life with a healthy, poised posture.*

Do with what you have. Executive Charisma isn't about your look but how you look at things and what people see when they look at you.

Regardless of your height or your physical appearance, you have to do with what you have.

"It's amazing to see how others react to you when you walk and sit and stand with good posture and a smile. It's not just about what you say but how you say it," says Chet Kapoor, vice president and general manager, BEA Systems.

Outside of lucky genes, good care, and surgery, the best thing you can do to help you feel confident is to hold yourself correctly and use "I'm adequate" self-talk. You'll be viewed as attractive. If you stand tall and straight and smile, you'll minimize the stooped shoulders and shrinking bodies of the stereotype of someone lacking success. The older you get the more difficult this is. As one man said, "I can't keep up with the trends but I can keep my posture. . . . I work out to cultivate a presence. I want to stand straight to both attract and intimidate."

According to *Psychology Today,* one in six men would like to be taller. Standing straight and tall with good posture makes you *appear* taller.

Society discriminates in favor of tall people. If you're tall with good posture, you're viewed as confident, vital, disciplined, proud, youthful, dignified, and joyously alive. If you're short with good posture, you're viewed as having those same positive attributes. If you're tall or short and slouched, you're viewed negatively as scared, a loser, sheepish, shameful, guilty, worried, and lacking self-acceptance, control, and discipline.

One Monday night football commentator said, "The players' posture and body language tell you all that you need to know about the score." That's for both the winners and the losers.

Security experts tell you to avoid the person standing in a crowd with rolled shoulders posture, especially if they have a nervous look, because they are the dangerous ones. The person with the "hidden" agenda has the hunched-over look.

Slouching restricts breathing, decreases circulation, and keeps stale carbon dioxide in your lungs longer. So, regardless of your parent-given height, stand tall and straight.

It's interesting that your Executive Charisma makes you appear taller. People who are admired are viewed as "bigger than life." How many times have you seen a politician or celebrity and said, "I thought he'd be taller." The most frequent comment from viewers of the lifelike reproductions of famous people at Madame Tussaud's Wax Museum is, "I'm surprised how short they are."

Height is relative. A bank executive friend is 6 feet 6 inches tall. He says he didn't realize what his height did to others until he started hanging around with some NBA players who made him feel short.

If you're already a tall person, all the more reason for good posture. More people will see you anyway because they can.

"A candidate needs to be 'alive' there in front of me. A combination of posture, some hand movement, where they're really listening, and some energy comes out of their body." That's more important than their looks, said a headhunter.

One executive told me about a person who works for him: "He is the person in the meeting whom you don't even know is there. He is very quiet, doesn't smile, is stoic, offers no body movement, hunches, and talks softly. It's too bad, because he is extremely bright, has incredible insights, and smart things are going on in his head all of the time."

Regardless of height, weight, hair (or lack of), age, and looks, make the most of what you have by living "straight."

Lift up, suck in, and breathe. Whether you're sitting or standing, for good posture: (1) pull yourself up by lifting your rib cage away from your pelvis, (2) roll your shoulders back and down, (3) pull your stomach in at the belly button toward your spine, (4) breathe, and (5) maintain the posture and keep breathing.

To avoid thrusting shoulders back looking like chicken wings, place your thumbs toward you on your chest and run them up your breast bone over your collarbone and off your shoulder to lower the shoulder.

Caroline Creager, president of Executive Physical Therapy, says, "Work to strengthen your back muscles in your exercise routine for posture by pinching shoulders together." Oprah says, "Breasts to the sky, saluting the sun."

Another way to get your posture where it should be is to stand up against the wall with your head, shoulders, rear, and heels against the wall as much as possible. Holding that position, now, walk away from the wall and keep the positioning.

Hold your head as though it is a helium-filled balloon, moving, not rigid, but with alertness to look comfortable, confident, and competent. Have an imaginary string at the back of your head, but keep the chin level as though laying it on a shelf to elongate your neck.

For good posture while standing, flex your knees to help alignment. When you stand with your feet slightly apart and arms at your side, you minimize stress on your lower back and give yourself endurance as well as a look of confidence and comfortableness.

Breathe to release tightness from trying too hard. Get the old air out of your lungs. With the good posture (stomach to the spine, shoulders back and down), relax and let the air come in, preferably through your nose. Repeat: sigh out for a count of four; relax your diaphragm in for a count of eight. Sigh out, relax in. Sigh out, relax in. (Stop and try it right now: breathe in for a count of four, out for eight.) You're re-educating your body with improved form to mentally and physically rebuild muscles to retain the form.

Standing up straight enhances your breathing, which increases energy, improves circulation, massages your inner organs, makes for a healthier heart, clears out the stale carbon dioxide in your lungs, improves your digestion, and oxygenates your brain, all of which helps lower your stress levels. "Standing up straight is one of the most important things you can do," says Alison Toth, M.D., director of Women's Sports Medicine Program at Duke University Medical Center.

You may have to remind yourself 101 times today to lift up, suck in, and breathe. Tomorrow it may be 99 times. Every day you keep at it, the more difficult it becomes, or at least, the guiltier you feel reverting to a sloppy, slouched posture. If you don't do this all the time, whether you're "on" or not, you lose the necessary good form. Then when you have to you can't. You don't succeed like the CEO who says about walking on stage before a live audience, "All of a sudden you see the crowd and suddenly your body takes a different posture—your stomach is in, your shoulders are back—and, oh my God! Boom! It starts."

Decide to live the rest of your life with a healthy, poised posture. Believe me, everyone who has good carriage works on it. No one just has it perfectly, naturally. It comes from training and habit. Accept the fact that it will take weeks, even months, to unlearn the poorer posturing you've allowed yourself to sink into from the years of carrying "the weight of the world" on your shoulders. And then it will take the rest of your life to keep at it.

Years of tension and stress combine to cause you to hunch your shoulders. On the outside you have rounded shoulders, drooping chest, head jutted forward, pelvis tilted forward, all of which creates a muscle imbalance. Inside, poor posture contributes to your tension and physical stress because it compresses your spine, squeezes internal organs, decreases lung capacity, and causes blood vessels to constrict. All that makes for chronic back or neck pain and headaches. Plus, slouching generally makes you feel depressed.

Readjust your posture 88 or 898 times a day as necessary. Give yourself a mnemonic device. For example, readjust every time you hear a noise: a honking horn, train whistle, computer sign-on, cough from the next cubicle, phone ring, and so on. Have it trigger you to readjust. Now hold your good posture for the entire length of a song. (Hold it for the entire length of your commute.)

To walk with your good posture (stomach to the spine, shoulders back and down, breathe) keep your toes pointed straight ahead. Look at your footprint pattern when you walk on the beach: Toes should be pointed straight ahead not out like a duck.

Let your arms swing freely, slightly forward and back with fingers curved as if you were carrying a role of quarters. You can sloppily slug around, or you can walk purposefully, showing that you have a destination and a certainty in how you're getting there. Geishas are taught to "walk like waves rippling over a sandbar." Don't worry about that for yourself; if you just get your feet to point straight ahead in the sand, it will be enough.

Pause when you enter a room, someone's office, a restaurant, or a party. Take a split second to adjust, breathe, and then walk in as far as you can.

When your arms are free at your side, you are able to move and gesture with them. Crossing your arms looks like you're "closed" to others, and hands in the pocket looks nervous. Keeping your arms behind your back with clinched hands looks military and rigid. As in everything I advise, choose the effect you want and take the subsequent physical action to support it.

Work sitting down is usually paid more than work in other positions (aside from rock stars). Since you'll be sitting a lot, do it right. Don't sit down as though you're grabbing a vacant seat in the subway. Don't sit hunched like an animal waiting for a blow.

To sit tall and straight, approach the chair, pause, and feel the chair with the back of your leg. Go straight down into the front of the chair and lower yourself with your good posture. Pause a second then smoothly move to the back of the chair if you want to "settle in"; otherwise stay "on the edge." You choose the effect. (To stand, reverse the sitting position. Get to the edge of the chair, with good posture, and "rise to the occasion.")

Women should cross their legs at the ankle or knee but keep their legs together. Don't let your ankles twist, turn, show the heel of your shoe, dangle, or wiggle. It looks nervous and not controlled. If crossed at the ankle, pointed left, the left leg should be in front to look poised. If crossed at the knee, pointed left, the right leg is the one that crosses over with toes pointed to the left together to look poised.

For men or women, keep your arms asymmetrically positioned—one on the arm rest, one on your lap—to look comfortable, confident, and competent. Avoid clasped, clenched hands or symmetrically placed hands—it looks as though you are nervous. Separated hands free you to gesture.

To avoid looking stiff and scared, you have to gesture when you're talking, sitting, and standing. Gesturing isn't some contrived affectation made for television. As early as 1806, there were books written about "gesture in oratory" describing "56 different gestures executed with either one or both hands, in straight lines or curved, with quick or slow movements to express humility, mockery, concession, sublimity, comfortableness, confidence."

A currently popular gesture is to point at people, with "chin tucked down and eyebrows raised," according to *The New York Times* magazine. The pointing gesture used to be impolite and reserved for pointing at the accused or the shamed. But gestures change over time and with cultures. The point is to positively indicate, "You're the man," "You've got it."

Gestures vary around the world. The same cupped hand, palm down, fingers and thumbs all touching means "What exactly do you mean?" in Italy, "That's just perfect" in Greece, and "Be patient" in Egypt.

To gesture effectively, align your words with your actions; then move your hands/arms from your shoulders, not your elbows or wrists. Your goal is to have coordinated gesticulations. Gesture asymmetrically—not boringly, nervously, identically, or with jerky nervous flailings of your hands and arms.

Keep your head level. When it is tilted to one side, you seem to be seeking approval or questioning. Tilting the head forward makes you look timid and weak. Tilting the head back makes you look haughty. Just keep it level as in "level-headed businessperson."

Limit the repetitive nodding up and down. You don't want to look like one of the bobbing-head toys they give out at the pro games. When you bob your head, you look nervous, trying to please, and anxious. Give one deep purposeful nod or a verbal nod, "I see" or "Okay."

"I have a friend who bobs his head a lot and I pick it up from him. When I go home my wife says, 'You've been talking with Jack today haven't you?" says one executive.

If you're around people who have good posture and gesture well, you will likely emulate them. But you're probably around people less aware and less disciplined than you, and so you have to set the example for yourself as well as for others.

When you "rise to the occasion" and prepare to leave a room, shake hands and pause. Don't hurry. It looks like you can't wait to get away. Take your time and replace/resituate the chair if you've moved it. Show some respect of the other person's space. With good posture, purposefully walk to the door. Before you exit, turn and nod goodbye again. Pause. Leave. Position the door as it was when you went in.

Don't just read through these recommendations for your physical actions, thinking (1) It's not that important, (2) I do it fine already, or (3) I'll try it later. Stop right now and take yourself through the right movements. You likely do it well enough, but why not do it near perfectly? Practice to see what it feels like when you aren't on the "hot" seat, so that it becomes second nature when you are.

HANDSHAKES

When Richard Maracinko, author of several books on the Navy SEALs, shakes hands, he uses two. The left is to check your pulse to see if you're nervous meeting him and then he acts accordingly.

A famous restaurant owner in New York lets people know what their status is with her based on her choice of greeting: Newcomers get a nod of the head, semiregulars get a handshake, regulars get a peck on the cheek, and the favored few get a stand-up kiss and hug.

Probably better than a *Time* magazine article that reported on a tribe in Papua, New Guinea, where men meet each other

continued

---

with a genial clasping of each other's genitals instead of a handshake.

The Center for Nonverbal Studies reports on the "latest" touch to seal the deal: the bump. That's what we witnessed when Michael Capellas of Compaq and his counterpart Carly Fiorina of Hewlett-Packard signed off on their merger proposal. We also see bumped fists on the athletic field, on television, and in the movies.

Say you choose to stick with the traditional good mutual handshake:

Start with your good posture when approaching the person. Pause before you reach out so as not to get too close too soon. Plus, it makes the handshake gesture feel special and directed to the person.

Clasp palm to palm. Women should pay particular attention to not letting their fingers be what the person grasps. Palm to palm helps avoid squishy shakes or painful ones with your fingers squashed.

Hold on a split second longer than necessary. Three pumps versus one. Retrieve your hand.

Check your distance: eighteen inches in New York, twenty-four inches in Cheyenne. You'll be disliked instantly if your distance is wrong. Adjust as necessary.

You can put your left hand on the person's wrist, elbow, shoulder, or even hug. Pelvises don't touch. Clavicles can.

continued

Bad technique is *too* sweaty, far away, close, late in the release, early in the release, high, low, many pumps, or few pumps.

The two-handed shake, hug, backslaps, pats on the back, pat on one cheek while kissing the other, bumps, grasps can be done with anyone at anytime based on the effect you want.

If you want to *avoid* being the recipient of a hug or hand kiss, get your arm/hand out on your approach. The person may still try it, but you've set the stage for the stiffer arm shake, and you'll more likely succeed in getting it. While you avoid the physical contact you don't wish to engage in, you still have to maintain the person's self-esteem and not leave the other person feeling rebuffed.

There are times you do not want to bond with the shaker. And you choose to do the opposite: Give a brief, brusque, flea-flicker shake, with no eye contact. Everything depends on the effect.

SMILE

Of all the physical behavior patterns expected of a leader, facial expression is the most telling. Before you utter a word, you (and others) "read" faces, put on a "game" face, "make faces," take things at "face" value. Your face conveys more about you than any other part of your body. Think about it. What do your shoulders, hair, waist, torso, and legs say? Next to nothing. The only other body part that is informative is the hands.

Your facial expression helps you climb the corporate ladder—or not. It's the first place people look to decide if they are going to like, trust, and remember you. A pleasantly professional expression makes you look like you are a thinker, helps you connect more quickly, gives credibility in your connection, and establishes a presence about you.

"I meet no strangers. I smile, with good eye contact. Give a firm grip, clasping their other hand on top with mine," says Jerome Davis, president-Americas, EDS Business Process Management. "I want to send a message that I want to get connected with you and I want to know you."

His attitude is the direct opposite to what a curmudgeon said, "I heard that what a mate wants most from you is a smile, so I start every day with one and get it over with."

Your face is involved in every interaction, and your facial expression is the most important thing you wear.

People conclude more about you from the look on your face than the words that come out of that face: confidence, assertiveness, reliability, nature, integrity, intelligence, creativity, and social ability. (Like photographs are worth a thousand words, so is your look.) Your choice of expression can make you appear to be a calm, happy, interacting, self-confident person that people want to do business with—or not. It causes you to look pleasant, comfortable, and approachable. It defuses hostility and draws people near you—or not. It's your choice. All it requires is a little use of some small muscles in your face. The same ones Clint Eastwood acts with!

The look of enjoyment *should* be a natural state. But it isn't. Go outside and take a fifteen-minute walk and look at the expressions on people's faces. They are awful. You see mad, sad, scared, nervous, serious, vacant expressions on 70 percent of the people. Another 20 percent look perpetually disagreeable, as if they never had a pleasant moment in their life and want to keep it that way! If someone does smile at you or looks happy, it's an oddity. And when you initiate a smile, you'll see some people literally try to fight back one as they feel it coming on. The only time some people seem to smile is when they prevent someone from getting onto the ramp of the highway.

"When people see you smile, they smile back and you get good energy," says my eleven-year-old friend Tsaia Edmonds.

In San Francisco I saw a panhandler in a wheelchair with one leg cut off below the knee and one leg cut off above the knee. He held up a sign that read. "Hi. Smile." And he was beaming at everyone who passed. If anyone had reason not to smile it was he, yet he was smiling.

If you're a rock star, you don't want to adhere to the smile advice. I know it will make you look beguiling and that doesn't fit the image. But for the rest of you, read on.

I've seen studies that reported higher-status people smile *less,* and I've seen studies that report higher-status people smile *more.* The truth is that research can be skewed to prove anything. The value of the research is to raise your awareness so you can make better choices. Your smile should be a refreshing expression of matter-of-fact-cheerfulness—about being alive—regardless of your current status.

The pleasant facial expression comes from attitude—which flows together from your integrity, confidence, full-disclosure approach, and Executive Charisma. It is not a smiley face, a smirk, a grin, a seeking approval look, or a beamish grin.

You will not enjoy every aspect of your work life, you will not make friends with everyone, you will not win every fight, you will not always be happy with your surroundings. A smile camouflages all of that. And, although you think you may be smiling "inside" from your soul, don't get too busy, too caught up to neglect to convey it on the outside.

Most everyone has a smile when something is pleasing to them. The key is to have it when you don't feel enthused. I know you don't always feel like smiling. So what? You have to do it anyway.

A time not to smile is for your police mug shot.

I know there will always be people suspicious of your smile. They're usually worried that you know something they don't. The truth is, you do!

People have actually said to me, "I don't know how to smile. I don't know what I'm going to look like. I don't know if I'm smiling. I'm self-conscious about it." So here's how.

HOW TO SMILE

- *Relax your jaw, keep your lips apart, and turn up the corners of your mouth.*
- *Engage your eyes.*
- *Retain that expression all the time.*

Relax your jaw, keep your lips apart, and turn up the corners of your mouth. It may sound silly to teach adults how to smile, but then some seem to need to learn.

To relax your jaw start with relaxing your feet and follow with your whole body. You won't feel so much that you're smiling, but being smiled. To relax your jaw and keep your lips apart, say a word that is your own mnemonic device, such as cheese or Cheez Whiz or soufflé (which is what Julia Child uses to get the smile on her face) or blue cheese (as Tsaia suggested to me). Now keep the corners of your mouth slightly turned up, lifting your cheek muscles. The raised cheeks round out your face, soften it, and increase the blood flow that nourishes your skin.

You want a loose face but not a slack and "duh" looking one. A relaxed jaw isn't a rictus. (Yeah, I had to look it up the first time I saw that word too. It means a gaping grimace.) As you relax your jaw, slightly wobble it back and forth. Those muscles are really tight, aren't they? You need to get them looser, which starts by relaxing the jaw muscles.

Before politicians do their televised debate or Oscar nominees walk the red carpet, they practice their loose face. This isn't to be mistaken for a long face or deadpan look.

Lips apart, instead of compressed lips in a tight, tense line, gives a hint of a smile that should remain on your face at all times. You can still look concentrated but not constipated. Or like the French expression *la pluie qui marche,* which means "rain that walks."

Don't set your jaw like hardening concrete, scowl, frown, grimace-and-bear-it, or furrow-your-brow creating glabella lines, or "cleavage for your forehead" (as one comedian put it). Cease clinching your teeth. A deeply furrowed brow and dour, morose countenance, acting with a professional gloom, is not a mark of wisdom. You look scared, worried, stressed, and a little like a shar-pei puppy.

The face has forty-four muscles and roughly 7000 different possible facial expressions. Your smile engages at least three major muscle groups to increase blood flow to your face, helps create a healthy glow, and tones your facial muscles. It increases antibody-producing cells and activates virus-fighting T- cells. It also causes positive physiological changes in your body, such as an increase of mood-elevating endorphins and a reduction of cortisol, a chemical that indicates stress in the body.

One study reported that the physical effect is the same whether the smile is faked or not. Your body doesn't know the difference, but the physiology takes over and the result is the same. (The field of research is called *psychoneuroimmunology,* which defines the communication links and relationships between our emotional experience and our immune response.)

Laughter tones facial muscles, sort of like an aerobic workout. And if you laugh so hard you "fall on the floor," you'll heal quicker because, as explained earlier, laughter boosts the immune system by increasing antibody-producing cells and activating virus-fighting T-cells.

If for no other reason, smile so your teenagers learn to also. That same study found that "women who smiled most in their college yearbook photos had happier lives, happier marriages, and fewer personal setbacks in the following thirty years."

Babies smile, on average seventy-two times a day. But as they grow up and get educated and socialized they withhold smiles. Like everything in this book too little or too much of anything becomes bad.

A smile not only increases the pleasantness in your face but also improves your voice quality by opening up the breathing apparatus of your larynx and esophagus. When you speak, the words come out in a richer, lower tone. Your mouth open a little bit increases your resonance. Try humming; you can't do it with a clenched jaw.

A rich, authoritative, relaxed sounding voice causes people to take what you say more seriously and generally respond more positively.

Your voice needs to have the same quality at the start of your day as at the end and during all the ups and downs in between. You don't want to allow leakage by showing irritation, impatience, anger, tiredness, and the rest, which causes others to view you differently than you want. I refer to this as the "pass-the-salt tone of voice." It's a reminder for consistency. Pass the salt is not a *sotto voce* so that people have to strain to listen nor is it *"pass*-the-salt" "pass-*the*-salt" "pass-the-*salt."* It's an even, engaged, clear tone with no hidden emotions or agenda. It's a safe-to-use tone for all situations.

You can retain variety in your pacing, volume, and tonality while still sounding comfortable, confident, and competent, with pass-the-salt delivery. People will listen because you aren't irritating, obnoxious, and/or out of control.

Airline pilots are taught to speak with deliberation, a folksiness, a down-home calmness as you ratchet back and forth in your seat. They say, "It might get a little choppy" in their pass-the-salt tone. Imagine the reaction if you heard, "It might get a little *choppy."*

A "low" voice can be a power play like yelling is, or it can stem from shyness, politeness, nervousness, and so on. Regardless of the emotional reason, use a consistent, calm, cool, collected, easily audible tone of voice.

Don't speak so low that people have to strain to listen to you. Make it easy for people to hear and understand you. A vice president in the computer industry was described by his boss, "I had to turn up the volume three times during one phone call with him." The same vice president explained to me, "To convey authority I lower my voice, speak in a lower tone." It didn't convey authority; it created miscommunication on many levels.

With a diverse workforce composed of various cultures, races, creeds, with foreign expressions and words, all the more reason to speak so you're heard and understood—not misunderstood.

Sometimes people yell out of fear, frustration, anger, and ignorance. Even when they raise their voices though, you don't. Stay on the pass-the-salt level. You don't need to succumb to an emotional display and fight fire with fire. Even if you are just as scared, frustrated, and angered, don't also be ignorant and yell back.

When you speak, smile. Eryca Dawson records informational messages for directory assistance at Verizon. She says her secret is, "I smile when I speak, even if I'm saying, 'I'm sorry, the number you called has been disconnected.'"

Engage your eyes. Smile with your eyes. Put thought into the statements you make with your eyes. A smile without the eyes and the eye contact is disengaged. The eyes are how you talk along with the smile before you actually open your mouth.

Engaging your eyes—and the eyes of the people you're talking to—sends a message of sincerity and trust in your communication. I remember one CEO telling me in awe about meeting a celebrity CEO, "He gave me direct eye contact and held my gaze for a while as he completed a thought. He seemed to look at me more often than the other CEOs at the meeting."

The benefits of engaging your eyes are both emotional and physical. First, a smile on your face causes a radiant attractiveness. Second, even the slightest smile makes your eyes moisten thus giving a sparkle, a luster, and a brightness (same physical reaction as a yawn).

Think about how you use your eyes when you're mad at someone or attracted to someone. There's quite a different "glimmer" between the two.

The best eye contact is looking someone straight in the eye and speaking. In the most tense, nervous situations you find yourself in, you need to use straight eye contact more than anything. It takes courage, but it also generates trust and sincerity.

When you talk to people, you can occasionally look at their noses and mouths to appear to be looking in their eyes. It feels the same to them but takes a little pressure off you without giving you the appearance of "shifty" eyes. Try it out with a friend. Give the person the same ten-second spiel looking at his or her mouth and then at the eyes. Ask if the person can tell where you were looking. An advantage of looking at people's mouths is that you are literally reading their lips when they are talking to doubly add to your understanding of what they are saying. Also, if the person you're talking to doesn't have good eye contact or has a "floating eye," you can maintain your own with the person anyway.

Turn your head to face people. If you look at them without face forward, it looks a little sneaky, as though you can't "look 'em in the eye." Minimize looking up at the ceiling or down at the floor. Better to look horizontally, over their shoulders. Your head remains level, you're not darting away, and you give yourself a second to pause, and then speak.

Wandering eyes equate to a wandering mind. Steady eyes imply that—steady. Hollow, deer-in-the-headlight and closed eyes are all behaviors that people will read and will give a negative view of you.

One company president told me about a former colleague of his "who would say something in a meeting and his eyes would dart from person to person looking for approval and reassurance as to what he just said." Later this executive was accused of misappropriation of corporate funds. It's worth noting that thieves and criminals know to dart from person to person and to *not* make a connection. They don't want people to register them in their minds and more likely be remembered. Criminals don't want that. You do.

I heard about a Hollywood mogul who required all assistants to avert their eyes when they passed him in the hallway. That dictate had to be a superficial power play stemming from his own insecurity. You should never allow yourself to work for such an individual much less be that individual.

Regardless of how people treat you, keep a relaxed smile and look them in the eye.

Retain that expression all the time. People who go in for plastic surgery could save themselves a lot of money and pain if they just focused on their facial expression. Your broad smile and engaged eyes are your best secrets for physical attractiveness, at any age. At the very least, it saves you the cost of expensive makeup and the time to apply it.

The National Science Foundation results found that women smile more than men. Good for us! Regardless of whether you are a male or female, a smile is an instant "facelift" for you and the only thing that looks good on your face when you're old.

Don't mistakenly think facial expression discussion is tailored to or reserved for women. It isn't at all. The best leaders of both sexes know to keep an energetic, awake, alert, alive expression despite how they feel.

Think about your own expression, now, when you're reading. It's probably not the same one you give when you're listening to your boss describe a new project—but then again, it should be! Practice your Cheez Whiz while reading, watching television, driving, and so on. If you don't practice when it doesn't matter, you'll slip back into bad habits when under pressure and it *does* matter. Also, unless you keep your smile on your face all the time when you switch back and forth between having it and not you look fake, insincere, and *ungen-uine*—despite how you really feel.

Now that you know how to improve your smiling ability, use it.

You have to talk and listen with a smile. If you don't, it looks as though you think things are interesting when you are doing the talking but not so when others are doing the talking.

Smile even if you think your teeth look crummy or your face has looked funny since your first loose tooth. If your smile is dingy, then there is an entire industry that has sprung up to aid you: porcelain veneers, power bleaching, whitening pastes, whitening brushes, and white strips.

Greet every human being you encounter with a smile and return theirs if they happen to give it first. Like Tsaia said, when you walk around giving a smile, you'll likely get it back. Your power is to send others what you want to get sent back to you.

Try it, it's smile Ping-Pong. Now give a frown, you'll likely get one back. It's scowl Ping-Pong.

Frequently people tell me, "I'm so focused in my thinking and not even aware of how I look and the fact I'm grimacing or frowning," or I hear, "I just don't have the energy to smile at everyone I see. Plus I don't think it matters that much because I'll never see most of them again." Change that thinking and behavior.

A good time to turn up the juice in your smile is when you're in the hospital. I know, it's exactly when you don't feel like it. But if you put the little extra effort in, from my informal research, you'll get better treatment. Why? The nurses will respond more promptly to you because they know they won't face another grumpy person. The medical team stops by more frequently too. Your guests enjoy visiting because you look like you're getting better. And, you just might get better, faster.

Smiling is something you can control, blushing, on the other hand, is a bit more difficult. Take consolation in the fact others suffer this also, so much so that there is even a support group called the Red Mask Foundation.

With Cheez Whiz a blush is more likely to be ignored, dismissed, or not even noticed. Without it, it's amplified.

A blush is just a slight reddening of your complexion because the veins near the surface dilate from certain neurological signals. Your face stiffens, and a sensation of electric heat surges up your neck, cheeks, and ears. At the extreme, your eyes fixate, your voice speeds up, and confusion and loss of focus may result. Simultaneously, other peripheral vessels contract, causing clammy, cold, white hands.

The neurological signal can come from someone asking you a question, having to stand and speak, having a horn honked at you, someone making a snide comment or gesture toward you, people publicly singing Happy Birthday to you, or even some just recognizing you. Your reaction is part physiology and part psychology, which helps explain Mark Twain's comment, "Man is the only animal that blushes. Or needs to."

Experts say you can help minimize blushing by giving up caffeine, trying breath-control techniques, makeup, Prozac, or Valium. There is special surgery done in Sweden where certain nerves are severed in the chest running along the spine, called *endoscopic thoracic sympathectomy,* or ETS. Regardless of what you do, you will blush less as you get older.

Don't blush as I tell you, "A smile is the second best thing you can do with your lips."

PHOTOGRAPHS

A photo is around a long time, plus, in seconds, it can be transmitted around the world via digital photography and the Internet. Good spontaneous photos don't just happen. You need to think it through in advance so you have the photo-readiness—not the photophobia—that delivers the message you want.

I saw comedian George Carlin during a promotion tour of one of his books. When people asked to be photographed with him he agreed, and in every shot would hold his hand in a "thumbs up" gesture toward the other person. It instantly animated the photo plus maintained the self-esteem of the person by making it look as though Carlin was giving him or her thumbs up.

A friend of mine talked about her friend Carly Fiorina. "During Compaq negotiations she didn't want to be photographed, but she was aware that she was anyway. She held her head high, maintained a slight smile so when it happened it turned out favorable." Later I read a quote from Carly Fiorina, CEO, Hewlett-Packard, "I'm a very deliberate person. It doesn't mean I'm infallible. But deliberate. Very little happens by accident."

If you have to have one done, you might as well take action to ensure the photo sends the message you want.

At an event, size up the area and move to where the photo has better background and lighting. Light facing you, not behind you, is better so that you don't look "shady."

Button your coat jacket to appear neater and conceal your stomach hanging out. Turn at a slight angle, it's more flattering

continued

to the camera's eye than straight on. Have an arm bent at the waist slightly away from your sides (like you were holding a drink) to look relaxed, even though it doesn't seem more relaxed.

Don't be holding a drink in your hand, even if it's water. To the photo viewers you're a "drinker," a party person. It becomes your "history" because it's in print, and it sticks in their heads. The cliché "a photo is worth a thousand words" is true.

Reach out and touch another person in the photograph if possible. But keep your posture erect and don't slump or lean on someone or something.

Widen your eyes, make your neck longer, but also lower your chin and put your head like sliding it on a shelf so the photo shot isn't up your nose. Push your face forward slightly to jump into the picture. Keep your head level.

Look the photographer in the eye (even though you can't really see the person's eyes). The famous paparazzi, Ron Galella, said, "Eye contact makes for a good picture."

Have a comfortable smile and engage your eyes. Say "Cheez Whiz."

If it's a formal setting with a professional photographer think through what you want as a finished photo; don't just rely on the photographer posing you. Prior to the session review business publications you read and pay attention to photographs of executives. Think how different poses, dress, backdrops, and so on, affect you. Tear out and give samples of the ones you're impressed with to the photographer. It's more efficient for him or her to see what you have in mind.

5

Be Human, Humorous, and Hands On

If you deal with people in a personable manner, they will be more receptive to what you are trying to achieve. A personable manner means relating to and communicating with people as fellow human beings, using humor and even physically touching them with respect and acceptance.

If you attempt other aspects of Executive Charisma without this step, you will fail. If you just do this without the others, you'll do pretty well. But you and I want to complete the Executive Charisma puzzle, so we do it all.

"Your title gives you one thing. The responsibility to take care of people who report to you," says Mark Gunn, vice president people, eMac Digital. "Be fair, right, and equitable to all people. That's all they want."

The combination of being human, humorous, and touchy

- Breaks down barriers erected by title, position, or role

- Needs no interpretation, has no difficult foreign dialect

- Provides instant communication

- Lays a groundwork for trust in relationships

- Connects with people and improves bonding

- Increases likeability

- Saves time in developing affinity

- Helps you get along with a wider range of people more quickly

- Enables you to reapproach as often as you desire

- Gets you through difficult situations

To not be human is to create barriers, complicate communication, decrease likeability, waste time, limit your scope of influence, and maybe even cause you to look phony, corrupt, and alienating.

Ritz-Carlton's customer service training states, "Elegance without warmth is arrogance." People can't be snookered. They can quickly tell the "nerds and turds" as one music company CEO puts it. "People look past the rank—past the epaulets—and look at the person's humanity."

You can't be like the person in a Denver restaurant who was overheard saying, "Have your people call my people. If you don't have any people, call my people and we'll get you some people. Then we'll do lunch."

People think business, particularly big business, is a huge, powerful, all-knowing, monolithic enterprise. Business is just human interactions in a social/political organization with money attached to it.

To get what you want is to help people get what they want. It all starts with you, dealing as one person to another, experiencing human behavior, human spirit, human error, human sacrifice, human triumph, human weakness, and the human emotion of life.

As I say throughout this book, to be successful, you have to initiate with everybody—all the time. You have to deal person-to-person not role-to-role (before they do) up and down the ladder.

Many people I talked with for this book brought up Sam Walton, founder of Wal-Mart. I was told he wasn't the smartest in a room but he had a quiet confidence. When he spoke he was credible at every level. He could pull up a box on a dock and sit talking with dockworkers as comfortably as he'd don a grass skirt and do the hula on Wall Street. As the *Harvard Business Review* writes, "His dance signaled that he was a down-to-earth guy who didn't have an inflated view of himself . . . thousands of salespeople on the floor were as important as top executives."

When the company got to $100 billion he had a meeting and announced, "We just went out of the retail business. With 30 million coming in our stores a day, we're in the people business. Anybody can put product on the shelves. We'll be the best in how we treat people."

As Walton would talk, he'd show a little human foible. He'd drop his eyeglasses or pen or piece of paper. One assistant saw him do it so often he volunteered to carry the pen, paper, or whatever was needed for Walton. Whereupon Walton responded that he was just doing it for effect, to look less intimidating, even admitting, "I work at it."

BE HUMAN

We're all the same—we share common ground. It is very easy to get so caught up in our own importance, goals, responsibilities, fears, emotions, frustrations that we forget there are about eight billion people on the Earth with similar and possibly the same goals, responsibilities, fears, emotions, frustrations. People are just people. Everyone has a life. We should remember to never act that important when we aren't that important.

When I write this, you likely pause a minute and think, "Yeah, you're right, wow" and then go back to concerning yourself with your own needs and wants. That's only human. Pause again and think about others a minute more. Others being your significant other, colleague, spouse, parent, subordinate, boss, boss's boss, clerk at the grocery store, toll booth operator, grandmother, client, office jerk or jerkette, or anyone else. Consider what some of their goals, fears, frustrations might be.

"There is no difference in how I relate to people. The human way and the professional way is the same," says John Krebbs, CEO, PAC. "There is no game playing but there is a sense of fun and fair play."

Another CEO said, "I treat a fellow CEO and a waiter the same."

The people of the world, like you, want to improve . . . want to avoid pain . . . think about death . . . feel hectic and overworked . . . fear losing their money . . . have their eye on some luxury item . . . want to do right by their kids . . . love someone . . . like bargains . . . want to be understood . . . want to be talked to like a friend and an insider . . . have good days and bad days . . . like to have a good time . . . want to be treated fairly . . . have a jerk/jerkette to deal with . . . use their birthday, anniversary, or home address for their security codes . . . have their routine of where they go, who they see, what they do when they arrive . . . forget important items when they pack . . . aren't terribly fond of their looks . . . are proud when their children go into the family business . . . stare at rainbows . . . were horrified by 9/11 . . . brag about their children's accomplishments . . . don't like to think about boys dating their teenage daughters . . . want to be understood and loved despite their hard shell . . . are dissatisfied with their hair . . . wonder if they have what it takes . . . want world peace . . . feel frustrated . . . succumb to bargain traps . . . feel pressured . . . have everything seem to go wrong . . . have a family . . . want peace . . . are fearful of losing their jobs . . . feel insignificant . . . bleed red . . . fail . . . are speechless and occasionally lose every ounce of confidence . . . want to matter . . . want to live a long and happy life . . . want to be safe . . . want to laugh . . . want to be appreciated . . .

The above is true with people in Chechnya, Cuba, Wisconsin, Paris, Luxembourg, Bangkok, and Denver.

A high school football team in Colorado invited a high school football team from New York for a preseason exhibition game. One player from Colorado said about his New York peers, "They are so much like us but different."

A band member at a Hollywood celebrity wedding said about the couple, "They were just regular people except wealthier and prettier."

Kenny Rogers expresses it in song, "Everyone needs three things in life: someone to love, something to do, something to look forward to."

What is most personal is most general. As the advertising copy reads for a new alcoholic beverage, "Here's to the differences that make us all the same."

Aside from our fingerprints, where no two people in the world are alike, we're pretty similar. Thank goodness for those unique prints! Your appearance changes with age, accidents, disease, weight gain or loss, plastic surgery, but your fingerprints don't change. Even identical twins have different fingerprints.

The point is we are all alike regardless of the paths taken. Repeatedly remind yourself of it so you consistently deal human to human.

HUMAN ERROR

When people make a mistake they proclaim, "I'm only human." Well that's true, but if it's you, a charismatic executive who makes the mistake, swiftly, genuinely, and thoughtfully deal with the blunder.

You don't always have to be right, but you do always have to take responsibility for being wrong.

UCLA coaching great John Wooden said, "You aren't a failure until you start blaming others for your mistakes."

Ensure that you are the only one who gets the blame. Don't suggest the problem lies in the interpretation and reaction, not in what you said. Don't excuse it as just your sense of humor. Don't blame it on some outside source, person, or metaphysical phenomena.

Relay your mistake to the person affected: your boss, board, spouse, and so on. Take responsibility and admit it in a sincere tone, "I was wrong and I'm sorry." Do not mistak-

continued

enly subscribe to some unwritten macho code prohibiting you from saying "I'm wrong."

If you're going to survive in the business world, you have to be up front when things go wrong, especially if you have the same customers over time. Go straight at it. Don't rationalize. Own your behavior. People will stick with you over the long haul if you deal with mistakes well.

Even if it's not one of those mistakes that "will take five years to forget," give all the bad news all at once and preferably early on. Don't wait until it's to your advantage. (One newspaper had a piece about Lanny Davis, who was President Clinton's spin doctor, "[Davis] made an art form out of the Friday night damage-control leak to wire service reporters so news would hit the Saturday papers, thought to have the least readership.") Delay only compounds the mistake. Do not misrepresent any information and cause a further apology. Acknowledge the pain you've inflicted. Don't act as though you're the one hurt even more by their reaction.

"To recover from gaffes, deal with them with humor and honesty. Depending on the situation, laughing at yourself eases everyone else and illustrates humility. If it is a serious gaffe, own up to it, be sincere in your regret of it, then recover well and move on," says Michael Trufant, CEO, ConnectUtilities.com.

Explain why it will never happen again. Make original mistakes, not the same one twice or the ones everyone else does, especially your predecessor.

continued

Do what you can to correct it. Stop feeling remorse and guilt. Don't repeat it. Then act like it is resolved; it just might be. Forget about the ones you can do nothing more about. As a professional ice skater was coached after she fell in competition, "Get your feet under and reset."

A few days later, if appropriate, make a phone call, send a note, or even a small gift to reemphasize your sincere apology.

If you are erroneously blamed for someone else's mistake, correct the misinformation right away. Set the record straight and put an end to false rumors. Don't be defensive and don't take it personally, but do take action.

"Whenever you're wrong admit it. Whenever you're right shut up," Ogden Nash.

HOW TO BE HUMAN

- *Cease dealing role to role and seek affinity.*
- *Act with affinity when others don't.*
- *Don't overdo it.*

Cease dealing role to role and seek affinity. Forget titles, roles, power, or position. You're just one down-to-earth human being interacting with another. Don't be distant. Touch with "heart, soul, and mind" regardless of rank, race, creed, color, or power.

"First and foremost we're humans. It's the human condition that binds us," says Kerry Hicks, CEO, HealthGrades, Inc.

Treat the person you're dealing with the way you want to be treated. Don't even hint of an attitude like the former manufacturing executive who was heard saying, "I'll have my objects call your objects." Or like the software CEO who walks up to the elevator, waits beside you, and doesn't talk. Or like the one who operates "in a suit of armor controlled by handlers."

Take a minute and reflect on the similarities, not the differences, between you and the person you're talking to. You don't want to be talked about with a comment like, "He never puts himself in my shoes."

Do like one CEO does: "I become that person."

"The first thing he did when we met was to create a connection between us. He tried to quickly relate to me and instantly make me comfortable," says Don Gulbrandsen, CEO, Gulbrandsen Technologies, upon meeting a legendary CEO.

I know depending on role, age, experience, and interests there are dissimilarities between you and others. Just because I'm from Kansas and you are from Kansas doesn't mean we're identical.

Still, there are more similarities than dissimilarities. Seek out common areas with questions. Try to find out more about the person you're talking to, not just about their business.

"In conversations with potential clients sometimes half of our conversation is about children. Why? If our value systems are aligned, they'll be inclined to work with me. Plus they let their hair down and we bond on a personal level. That's how I get comfortable with people and they get comfortable with me," says Mike Nieset, Partner, Heidrick & Struggles. When social values are shared you have an improved chance of success.

Judiciously volunteer information and reveal things about yourself to keep a comfortable balance of give and take. Initiate with questions first and foremost about them, their interests, their work, and their family. You develop affinity when you share common experiences. Don't wait for them to discover it. The questions in Chapter 3, which are designed to help you get to know a person, work well.

Without affinity there is no trust; with it there is. If people feel a camaraderie, they will go out of their way to work with you on an issue.

Talk face to face with people when possible instead of relying on chain of command, email, or phone. You're able to look them in the eyes and read their faces just as they'll be able to do with you.

"I try to move relationships outside the office setting, turning a business relationship into a personal one. For example, a German client was here for a two-week stay with his family. I took them all to my golf club for the July Fourth cookout and fireworks. It was a truly American celebration they had never seen before, and probably will never forget. Now our work has a whole new level of candor," one director said.

Act with affinity when others don't. Go out of your way to relate to others before you're comfortable.

If you are going to eventually be "human" with a person anyway, start out that way to (1) save time and (2) be genuine. People's gut impression of you is based on what you show them from the first contact.

One executive told me, "I don't do anything special. I don't plan it, manipulate anything, or try to figure things out in advance. I just be myself." That is a fine approach as long as it doesn't mean you can forget to maintain esteem, ask questions, ask favors, and so on as you're being yourself. If "be myself" is your code for being lazy in interpersonal relationships, that is not all right.

You need to relate on a human level even when others don't. Everyone should get the same treatment from you, not just the ones who "count" or are readily likable themselves. Do it with the ones who test your conviction, who don't respond as you think they should, as well as the receptive ones—higher and lower in the organization.

"The customers who are the most impressive and memorable are the friendliest to us, the waiters, as well as their meal companions. They remember names and some detail from previous encounters. The people waiting to meet up with the big-shot customer frequently treat us like dirt. Then the big-shot customer comes in, greets us, and gives a hug and a kiss. It's funny to watch the reaction of the ones who weren't very nice. They are shocked at the respect given and then they try to grovel and make up for their earlier snootiness," says one restaurant maitre d'.

Whether in a business or personal exchange, people remember you in a positive way if you are easy and proactive in trying to connect.

Don't overdo it. Don't get overly personal. Being human doesn't mean you initiate inappropriate intimate exchanges. It's not a license to invade privacy.

You obviously use common sense in not speaking about body functions, marital intimacies, things done in the past. But don't let the fear of saying something wrong inhibit you from saying what could be and should be said in an attempt to build rapport.

Being human does not give you license to "wear your emotions on your sleeve" or take things personally. Don't prematurely react to something someone says or does until you've found out their reasons for saying or doing whatever they did that bothers you. Ask, and ask again until it is clear. You don't have to like the answer but at least get as close to the truth before you choose how to react. Taking action based on your emotional assumptions does not follow anything recommended in this book.

A complaint I frequently hear from men about women colleagues is that they take things personally when it's "just business." Of course things are personal. It's one human being interacting with another human being. If both are doing all they can to expect and give acceptance to maintain self-esteem and not try to injure the other mentally or physically, that's good personal exchange. Bad personal exchange is taking action to take advantage of, mess over, hurt or harm you and/or your career.

Give people the benefit of the doubt just as you want it. Receive their action with the optimistic perspective that they are acting with integrity. Remember that just because the person doesn't do exactly what you want doesn't mean he or she is trying to "get you." Few people will ever "get you" more often than you allow yourself to "be gotten." If there is real evidence of it, ask about it in full-disclosure fashion to clear it up.

"Unless they are holding a gun to my head, nothing is that personal," one CEO told me.

It bears repeating that anything good taken to the extreme becomes bad. "Humanness can be a double-edge sword. It can make people feel comfortable and make people feel uncomfortable," says Richard Torrenzano, CEO, The Torrenzano Group.

It's right and necessary to be human; it's not good to be inappropriately personal.

You can be personable without taking things personally or making things personal. You can be friendly but you don't have to be friends. Don't overplay or underplay the human bond.

There's a little voice that speaks up inside of you when you're going over the line. Listen to it, adhere to it. Kathleen O'Donnell, partner, Advent, understands where that line is: "I let people feel that I know them, and they are not looked at as though they are strangers. I joke around about things we have in common and talk a little about things people in business don't talk about—like Harry Potter movies. And that's it."

HOW TO REMEMBER NAMES

You probably like to hear your name favorably called out. Well, so do others. People never forget that you remembered.

It's funny; the same guy who says he can't remember names remembers the Tennessee/Florida football game score in 1991 or the wine he drank in Tuscany two summers ago. Why does he remember the score? He watched the game so he heard the score (over and over). He talked about it with his buddies after the game, repeating the score. He read the newspaper articles about the game the next day, seeing the score again.

Why did he remember the name of the wine? He read the label when it was placed on the table, sniffed the cork, maybe even saved the cork and soaked the label off for his scrapbook. Later he shopped for that specific wine at the market, repeating the name to the clerk. The steps required to remember anything are hear it, repeat it, read it, use it.

To remember names, it is first of all important to make sure you hear it. As one person said, "As soon as he told me

continued

his name it went in one ear and out the other." Despite the fact you have a million different things going on in your head, have the person's name go in one ear and stay there.

When you introduce yourself to others, you generally hear only your own name. No wonder you don't remember theirs. When they say it, right then clarify the pronunciation if it's unusual and verify it. "What is your name, again, slowly?" Or if you heard it clearly the first time, "It's Seth, right?" To further associate the person and the name you can ask a question such as "How do you spell that?" "Is that a family name?" or "What inspired that name?" If there is a story, people like to tell it.

Some people are particularly sensitive about the pronunciation of their names. People named Susan don't like to be called Suzanne. Elaines don't want to be called Eileen. Kathays don't want to be called Kathy. Michaels may not like Mike, just as Roberts may not like Bob, and so on. It takes little effort to get it right, so do.

If you get the person's business card, look at it and read the name. Tying the visual with the audible doubles your chance of remembering. Add a note on the back about something you learned about the person in the conversation, the "do list" item you want to follow-up with for the person, or some distinguishing characteristic.

"What works best for me is to visualize the spelling of the name, letter by letter. I usually remember faces with no

continued

problem, so it's about trying to visualize the name written next to the face," says Yvonne Hao.

Use the person's name to introduce him or her to another person. State the second person's name clearly, so it increases the chance of the first person hearing and remembering it also.

When I'm walking my dog on the bike path and people stop, chat, and bend down to pet him, I'll volunteer, "His name is Scooter," and inevitably the person will say, "Scooter, you're a good dog . . . or Scooter, you're a cute dog." And when we depart, they'll usually say "Good-bye Scooter." Then weeks later I'll run into the same people and they'll say, "Hi Scooter." They remembered the dog's name because they repeated it so many times.

When you meet a person again, volunteer your name to make it easy on them whether you do or don't remember theirs. Preferably you can say, "Roger, nice to see you, Debra Benton," as you extend your hand to shake with a smile on your face. If you can't remember his name, you can say, "Hello, I'm Debra Benton," pause and shake. He'll likely volunteer his name. This time make sure you register his name in your memory so you do remember next time.

If you're with someone who can't remember the name of someone you are both meeting, you can be the one to initiate an introduction with, "I'm Debra Benton, this is my friend Kristie." Then pause and let the person say his name.

continued

You end up making it easier and smoother for both of them (a two-for-one maintaining of esteem!).

By the way, at a meet and greet when you wear a name tag, place it on your right shoulder, not your left. It's easier to read when people shake hands with you because they can see it and therefore remember. I saw a man in a wheelchair put his name tag on his hat to make it easier to read. The worst are name tags on neck chains that hang around your chest or drop below; if you are a well-endowed female this causes men and women to study your bust area to see your name.

BE HUMOROUS

Notice how similar the words human and humor are? It's not just the spelling that's close but also the benefits derived. Humor is the ultimate in being human. They are totally interrelated. Only 15 percent of humor comes from jokes. All the rest comes from the laugh of recognition of "I know how you feel" from human experience.

When you inject a little levity, causing a laugh, it makes you happy. Likewise, when you make other people laugh they're happy. You can laugh, kid around, poke fun and still be seasoned, wise, and understanding of the world.

It's okay if you aren't funny but it's better if you are. Many people tell me some version of, "I like humor. I have a good sense of humor. I enjoy a good comedian. But for myself, with people, I'm not that funny. I'm not a funny guy at all really."

Being humorous doesn't require a repertoire of one-liners. It means being of good cheer and willing to look at the irony and humor in all of us and in all of life.

"Moving from an engineering position to management I looked around at the most effective charismatic people in the company. I found they saw humor in everything. I could also see how it diffused conflict and it snapped everybody to," says a manufacturing organization market manager. "So I started working on my own. I'm not that good yet, but I'm better than I was." That's all I ask of you.

You may feel that there is an inverse relationship between moving to the top and retaining a sense of humor. That's not so. Research shows that business leaders who achieve the best results get people to laugh three times more often than do the mediocre leaders, according to Daniel Goleman, Ph.D.

Children laugh 300 to 400 times a day compared to adults, who laugh 15 to 18 times a day. Men laugh more than women. Women laugh more when men are talking than vice versa. Speakers laugh more than listeners. There's more laughter in a group than in a one-on-one meeting. Even evil people like to laugh. Humor is human.

Think about Super Bowl game advertising. Commercials promote a product usually in a humorous way. They say or do something all viewers can relate to; then they put a humorous spin to it. What a wonderful service those advertisers provide: in a thirty-second spot they have hundreds of millions of people around the world chuckling at the same time. How great is that?

The benefits of being human that I listed at the start of this chapter bear repeating. Being human helps you

- Break down barriers erected by title, position, or role

- Provide instant communication

- Lay a groundwork for trust in relationships

- Connect with people and improve bonding

- Increase likeability

- Save time in developing affinity

- Get along with a wider range of people more quickly

- Reapproach as often as you desire

- Get through difficult situations

- Avoid misinterpretation as it has no difficult foreign dialect

Humor provides all that. In addition it helps you

- Hasten the speed of an upbeat climate

- Create an environment with a sense of normalcy

- Face problems

- Keep people in a positive emotional range

- Help people do their most productive work

- Minimize intimidation

- Use another bonding gesture

- Maintain a sanguine façade; an equanimitous exterior

- Diffuse anger, fight despair, lessen pain

- Release tension at the end of a disagreement

- Increase your tolerance for uncomfortable situations

- Have the best defense against tears

- Have a relief from hostility and other uncomfortable emotions

- Change your perspective

- Increase feelings of confidence

- Decrease defensive criticism

- Minimize stress

- Solidify relationships

The next best thing to finding a solution to a problem is finding the humor in it.

As Bill Cosby says, "If you can laugh at it, you can survive it."

Author of *Swim with the Sharks* Harvey Mackay says, "Next to content, humor is the secret to reaching and persuading other people. . . . I especially like the stories that make me laugh for one minute and think for two."

Thinkers have more comedy in life. Robin Williams says his comedy is about stuff we've all gone through—the humanness is what's humorous—and that's not trivial or frivolous.

You can be serious but not take yourself, your looks, your (or others') title, or your existence so seriously. You can be intense but not tense. "I try to be very clear, organized, first, and then loosen up with a little humor, warmth, and candor. Punctuate firmness with moments of lightness. I don't want to create the illusion that this isn't serious, but it is more fun for me this way too," says Jeff Cunningham, CEO, Jeff Cunningham Partners, Inc.

One man told me, "I constantly remind myself that I don't work for the defense department and I'm not fighting a war day in and day out so I don't have to take anything too seriously."

Humor nuances vary between cultures, but universally everyone wants to and needs to laugh. And they want to laugh at any age. No laughter is undignified. (Well, giggling can be a little.) Yours might be polite and restrained or booming from the belly; regardless, it needs no interpretation. Laughter is defined technically as "one short exhalation of breath chopped into staccato segments lasting about one fifteenth of a second each and spaced one-fifth of a second apart."

Physically, laughter raises your heart rate as much as aerobic exercise. Some doctors maintain that 100 laughs are equal to about a ten-minute aerobic exercise. Laughter fortifies the immune system, works the muscles in your chest, diaphragm, and lungs to stimulate your heart and blood flow. People laugh more when they are healthy, and they are healthy if they laugh more. And as one person put it, "You don't stop laughing because you grow old; you grow old because you stop laughing. It is bad to suppress laughter; it goes back down and spreads to your hips."

Whether laughter is feigned or *un*premeditated, the benefits to your body remain the same. Take a minute right now and start chuckling. Don't worry about the funny stimuli, just go for the laughter. In a minute, you'll lessen your stress, aid your digestion, and improve your mood. If you can't laugh, you aren't trying, or you're so angry or frightened about something that you won't let yourself. Dr. Madan Kataria of Bombay, India, developed a style of yoga with the purpose of creating joy. He spawned laughter clubs worldwide for the purpose of the physical act of laughter even if it isn't prompted by humor. (You could start your own personal, private chapter!)

The good thing about laughter is you don't have to have the keen sense of humor yourself, you can just respond to others. Laughter shows giving acceptance to others. Chuckle appreciatively because you should and it's good for you.

By the way, since it's healthy for *you* to laugh think of the favor you are doing for others by giving them a "healthy" moment too.

HOW TO BE HUMOROUS

- *Seek out humor.*
- *Practice humor always: Do it before they do and when others don't.*
- *Don't overdo it.*

Seek out humor. Humor takes some effort because it is serious business. So you have to look for it and go where it is. For instance, choose a comedy movie over a drama. Turn on the Comedy Channel's "stand-up shows." Hang around with people who have a flair for seeing the funny side of a situation. Spend some time with nine-year-olds. Browse cartoons in the newspaper or *New Yorker* magazine. Listen to country/western music (lyrics like "when the wrong one loves you right" and "I left something turned on at home" have to bring a smile to your face). Sit and reflect on some happy and fun times. Reminisce at gatherings of family or friends. Discuss with them funny things that happened during the day.

Do what you have to do to make things a little more fun. "There are people who are a lot more fun than I because I'm pretty focused and all business. So I hire people who are more fun to be around— more well-rounded," says one financial company president. "I'm a good manager, but people like working with the good-humored type, so I get my vision done through them."

Look for situations that spark a smile. When I talked with people for this book inevitably funny stories would slip into the conversation. Sometimes they made a point, sometimes they just brought a smile to my face, but they are examples of good humor:

- From a girlfriend describing a recent break up with her boyfriend . . . "I had just had a hysterectomy, returned to work and was fired, went to visit my boyfriend and found a cigarette in an ashtray at his house with lipstick on it. I called him and said, 'Either you've been burglarized by someone who wears lipstick or we're breaking up.'"

- From a department head about his new boss . . . "He apparently is dyslexic because when he's supposed to compliment someone else he ends up bragging about himself."

- From a CEO about an investment . . . "It's like when the laundry owner calls and says they lost your shirt but in this case *you* lost your shirt."

- From a CEO who was dinged $5 for cursing in a board meeting . . . "If hell and damn costs $5, hell I know $100 words."

- From a recruiter talking about an executive who resigned from the company . . . "It's like he was at a red light, the car's stopped, it was still running, and he got out and walked away."

- From an executive talking about a business problem, "It's like pushing a mule up a hill. You're on the wrong end of the animal and it's incredibly difficult."

Now, none of these may pass the test to get on *The Tonight Show,* but they bring a smile to your face and even a little chuckle. You, yourself, can relate to some of them as a fellow human being—having "been there/done that."

When you find something particularly memorable and potentially usable, write it down. Keep a journal of funny things you hear someone say or do. Commit them to memory and use them. Pam Lawlor, category leader, Quaker Oats, was telling me about a particularly stressful day on the road. She went to the hotel bar and demanded, "Give me the strongest nonalcoholic drink you've got." That's a funny statement she came up with that could be used again in other situations. It's a clean comment for all audiences. You relate, having had stressful days yourself. You can visualize this attractive businesswoman bellying up to the bar and asking for the strongest drink—but nonalcoholic makes it funny. In eight words she's accomplished a lot of the benefits. Look for it, go where it is, and use it when you find it.

Practice humor always: Do it before they do and when others don't. If you wait until others engage in some humorous banter it's probably too late or awkward for you to get in. If you wait until someone else tries to reduce tension in the meeting by injecting some levity, you've waited too long. If you don't think it's your "place" to make people smile or laugh a little, first, you're wrong. If instead you just *go for it*, and try saying something that most can relate to in a humorous way, you are absolutely on target.

Practice your attempts in low stress situations, say, among friends and family. Then increase the stakes with people at work and then with the really intimidating people at work. If you don't practice, you won't develop the skill, and then even if something funny does come to mind, you're "goofish" in your delivery. Also, if you don't practice some delivery of good cheer all of the time, when you try some in an important situation, it will look out of character. You'll look fake, false, and as though you are trying too hard. It may still be funny, but the fact that it is so unexpected from you may mean that out of shock they can't even respond. Plus, consistency is something I've preached throughout this book. Everyone, in every situation, gets the same behavior from you.

The fact that someone else hasn't started with something humorous is because they are more cautious, less creative, shyer, or lazier than you. Don't wait. Don't hesitate.

When you initiate humor before others do, you show you expect acceptance and are human. The positive effect you have on others will help alter your own attitude toward it and cause you to try more. Do it even when you don't feel funny or feel like doing it. It's not about how you feel; it's about your effect on others anyway.

Use appropriate humor considering the audience, the relevancy, and the timing. Judicious good humor timed well before or after a meeting to stimulate trust and openness is good. If you burst in with something off the wall in the middle of someone's words, that isn't good timing.

Some humor is context sensitive. What one group likes another doesn't get. It's human to not always succeed. Johnny Carson did 4592 monologues, and not all of them were funny.

If you're not thinking, you can pick the wrong moment and look like you are sarcastic, cruel, or taking things too lightly; so don't pick those moments. On the other hand, do pick your moments to use humor to get people back on track. Once you've considered the timing, content, and context, forget about flopping.

It's nice if you're dealing with like-minded people. If you're dealing with a stuffed-shirt-serious stiff who's been cranky for ten years, your humor might fall on deaf ears. But you do it anyway because it's the right thing to do to be consistent; the humor makes *you* feel better; you might turn around some stuffed shirt; and it's good practice. Plus, people might be testing you, as discussed in Chapter 2.

With the influx of humor in your brain, pick and choose how you can use some of it at work. Insert a story, example, or analogy to support or make a point. Don't be disappointed if coworkers don't laugh uproariously. First, they just might be so surprised that you came up with something effective in breaking the ice or easing communication that they are stunned. Second, they could be foolishly trying to look and act so serious that they're afraid to show any reaction. Third, out of jealousy they don't want to help you look any better than you already are. They hope their nonreaction will discourage you from further good levity. And, fourth, they might be doing belly laughs under their breath and just don't know how much response to give because of their own insecurity. Regardless, assuming you're using good judgment, keep at it.

Despite all your forethought, your humor might be misinterpreted or misunderstood. It may backfire or bomb and you'll be embarrassed. So what? You just have to have an attitude of expect acceptance, smile, and have the courage to try *again*. Sometimes you just have to "go for it" because you'll look twice as silly in not going for it.

Comedy can be in the details of what you say or how you look: For example, a clever choice of words, the wit, the irony, combined with the eyebrow lift, the toe rise, the head and shoulder shrug may work. Any physical/visual overreaction, underreaction, or no reaction at all can work. Simply saying something ridiculous with a straight face can work.

Even a straight face can have a relaxed smile on it. And if your humor ends up misinterpreted, you minimize backlash if you simultaneously maintain a positive facial expression.

Sometimes not speaking is the best humor. Sometimes the silence is what's funny.

Unplanned, spontaneous humor is obviously good and endearing, but so is thought-out and rehearsed planned spontaneity. You can't always count on your quick wit. One big advantage of planning is that you can then test your humorous bit to see how it sounds before it actually comes out of your mouth. Stand-up comedy looks spontaneous but it's anything but that. It takes a lot of practice to get to the punch line of the bit with the right supporting facial expressions, hand gestures, body movements, words, and phrases.

The pros plan theirs. Jon Stewart of *The Daily Show* has a team of ten who go over the morning newspapers to cull potential bits. They also watch Associated Press video feeds. It takes a day to come up with the thirty-minute script. It's an all-day affair for Jay Leno to prepare his monologue. He looks at jokes, writes down jokes, reads jokes, and writes sketches. In the *New Yorker* magazine on average, 1000 cartoons are submitted a week for the fifteen or so slots. The submissions are narrowed down to fifty, which get presented to a team that divides them into piles of "yes," "no," and "maybe." The ones that get picked are the wry, understated ones. Then they are checked against an archive of previously printed cartoons, passed by legal review, and checked for accuracy in the drawing. Despite all the planning these people do, the result will not be 100 percent funny to everyone all of the time, just as yours won't be. As David Letterman says, "Every joke is a tough decision."

"Take aim at yourself and then pick your spots after that. You must earn the right to make fun of others by making fun of yourself," says Mark Katz, presidential comedy writer. Friendly digs can show inside relationships, but, in general, laugh at yourself not others. President Bush's speech team came up with this planned spontaneity, "I may mangle my words but I've never mangled the truth." It's a little self-mocking and self-effacing, which people like. Use this kind of humor at your own expense, never others'.

Pat Stryker, chairman, Bohemian Foundation, says, "My favorite saying is 'Blessed are those who can laugh at themselves for they will never cease to be amused.'" If you can't laugh at a joke about yourself, you probably deserve it.

It should be emphasized that humor, as it applies to Executive Charisma, is not joke telling. Sure occasionally you can repeat one you heard, but that's risky. Unbeknownst to them, one day in Denver, former Senator Alan Simpson of Wyoming spoke at one event and Governor Bill Owens of Colorado spoke at a different one. They both opened up by telling the same joke: something about a gas station attendant asking, "Did anyone ever tell you that you look like Alan Simpson (and for the other one, 'Governor Owens')? Kind of makes you mad doesn't it." The local paper reported the "sameness" of the joke in their coverage of the events, further embarrassing both.

"Telling stories seems to be a hallmark of charismatic leaders. My sense is that they do it better than others. It drives home their value to the organization as a whole and to people individually. People want to relate to an individual who deserves and has earned their respect, as opposed to an amorphous company," says one company's CEO.

Storytelling is different from joke telling. Stories are real; jokes are made up. Stories are yours, original, fresh, likely unheard, and less apt to be copied. With stories you make a point that people learn, remember, and visualize in a personal, passionate, purposeful way. Stories spark the imagination, tickle the funny bone, and share humanness.

The "setup" works for a joke or a story: Lock eyes, explain the situation, tell what action was taken, and tell what resulted.

When you have to explain something complicated, when you deal with numbers that numb, when you need to make a point sooner and more effectively, when you want to entertain, when you want your point remembered longer—stories work best.

A small problem with your stories is that if you embellish them over time, you may not remember what was previously used. If people hear a story again, they'll think you speak mistruths. So eliminate overused ones and tighten up new ones.

Use humor before others do and even if they don't. Use it with people closest to you, with strangers, and with business colleagues. Swallow your fear and take some action as Kate Hutchinson, senior vice president, marketing, Citrix Systems, says, "I allow the softer, humorous side of me to show even though it's vulnerable for me based on how I was raised."

Don't overdo it. I'm not recommending anything stupidly jokesterlike—being the court jester, wearing a red rubber ball nose, or other nonsense. This doesn't mean you can't mix some serious fun with frivolous elements. There are smart laughs, and there are dumb laughs.

"Yes" to humor that supports the human condition we all experience. "No" to sexually explicit jokes, ethnic jokes, or anything too mean about the boss, children, and death. I'm not promoting humor that is a dangerous flirtation with bad taste. Don't "play the fool," use slapstick, farce, screwball actions, or antics either. Refrain from putting your trash can on your desk and labeling it "in," or paging yourself over the intercom, or sending letters with no punctuation, or singing at the board meeting, or writing on the memo field of your checks "sexual favors." Those jokes would be sort of like stepping on a rake.

Humor comes from looking at something in a totally different way. Don't strain for a joke just for a joke's sake. The objective is to make the exchange flow with as much "human" and "humor" as possible.

If you just do the *opposite* of what is expected, traditional, or habitual, it's usually pretty funny. Occasionally go out on a limb and just try that alone with nothing else. That doesn't mean you have to do the special strut (like you see at football games after a score), wear something funny, or develop a stupid human trick. Although it's probably true what P. J. O'Rourke says, "Practically anything you say will seem amusing if you're on all fours."

It means stop and think "What's funny about this?" and then say that.

Being humorous is human. You "touch" someone with what you say to them, preferably providing a smile in addition.

TOUCH

In Executive Charisma, touch is both literal and figurative. It means to reach out, tear down defenses, and build a bridge with physical contact. If you want to lead in business, you have to touch. It takes courage, finesse, and a nonlascivious attitude. It encompasses the selective use of greeting gestures, embraces, air kisses, bumps, pats on the back, as well as plain and simple touching. You have to touch 'em all and the scary ones first and most.

You can use touch to pass praise, support, acknowledge, console, even correct. Good touch can make sad people happier and angry people calmer because it comforts and reassures—at least momentarily—erasing limits and lines. Effective touch, like smiling, posture, and good attitude, lifts depression, boosts the immune function, reduces stress, lowers blood pressure, and improves social relations.

Most people say to me, "I touch depending on my comfort level with the person." You can't wait until the "comfort level" is right; you have to initiate to get the comfortable relationship going.

One executive explained his technique, "I need an excuse to touch so I make sure I have a photographer at events. When he comes by, I use the opportunity to put my arm on the other person's shoulder and pose."

At the World Economic Forum in Davos, Switzerland, CocaCola CEO Doug Daft chatted amicably with PepsiCo CEO Roger Enrico. At the end of their conversation they embraced to the amazement of people watching. When a *Fortune* reporter asked about it, Daft said, "That was the first time I met Roger. We were talking and at the end of our conversation, I said, 'Let's embrace. That'll really get people talking.'" Still business competitors, Daft said, "You know, we're two human beings first."

Laying on of the hands shows your relationship is not just "tactical" but personable too. Politicians know to "kiss babies" but not hold them too long or they'll start crying and send the wrong emotional message.

"Human beings are wired for touch: the skin is the body's largest organ, covering almost twenty square feet and accounting for nearly one-quarter of the body's total weight. Touch is the first sense to develop in humans and is usually the last to fade. A daily dose of touch can be as essential to good health as diet and exercise," reports one study.

Saul Schanberg, professor of biological psychiatry at Duke University, says, "It is a preset pattern in mammals to need touching; it is not learned. But as humans grow, cultural cues tell us to keep our hands to ourselves. The actions might be gone, but the impulse is not."

One of Jack Welch's colleagues remembers a meeting in Paris for twenty-five to thirty customers, "It was at a very elegant club, and Jack spoke. Afterward he touched every customer. He called them by name, got into specific issues, thanked them for specific things."

Americans touch on average two times an hour. French touch three times more than Americans. Puerto Ricans touch 180 times an hour. Cigna Company found that babies who were held more frequently grew faster. The University of Pennsylvania found that your plants grow faster when they are touched. One scientific journal reported touch makes a plant more disease- and insect-resistant and makes it live longer.

There is inappropriate touch. I know that. The mistake you make in your desire to avoid a bad touch, though, is not to touch at all.

Like humor and human fit together so does touch. The key is in the right manner, in the right place, at the right time, and to be consistent with it when doing it.

HOW TO TOUCH

- *Have the right attitude; use good technique.*
- *Be consistent.*
- *Don't overdo it.*

Have the right attitude; use good technique. There will always be a touching taboo if your attitude or form is bad. I'm the first to say that if your technique or motivation is wrong *any* touch you give is bad.

Good form starts with the right intent—to bond, build rapport, give acceptance, maintain esteem, support, praise, and other positive intents.

Good technique is anything that doesn't make people feel uncomfortable or embarrassed. Then, initiate by extending yourself, pause, smile, breathe, give good placement, hold a split second, and withdraw.

Be close enough to the person, sitting or standing, so that you can comfortably connect. Touch people firmly above the waist such as on the shoulder, upper back, and lower arms.

When you grasp another (i.e., hug) you show intense emotion of agony, joy, or passion. Such a grasp expresses deep understanding where words won't suffice.

When you touch, don't hold too long or hard. And don't move your hands or arms into a rub. Nor should you touch others' pelvis, legs, chest, buttock, or belly (especially the pregnant ones).

"I put my arm around them and shut off the rest of the world," says John Krebbs, CEO, PAC. "Touch can be to bond, reward, or drive people away." Touch at a forty-five-degree angle toward their shoulders bonds, whereas the same touch given face-to-face, straight on, challenges people.

Touching someone can get you sued. But so can comments, looks, and lascivious thoughts. I know people hold back because of fear of being accused of sexual harassment. I am not suggesting in any way that touch is to be used to communicate an unspoken attraction to another. Don't cop a feel. Don't brush against. Don't rub.

Touch shouldn't come from an "urge." It's not a personal need but a personal gesture to show your openness and humanness.

If you make a mistake and accidentally touch someone in some place you didn't intend, apologize. Don't nervously ignore the unintentional misstep, clear it up right away without humor.

"I don't do a manly shake. Even if it's not politically correct I give a hug instead. I do it in an appropriate way, arm on their shoulder. If the person isn't close enough I reach and touch their hand. I've found the human approach is more effective," says Gayle Crowell, partner, Warburg Pincus.

The most commonly accepted touch is a handshake. The original purpose of the handshake was to show that two people were weaponless when meeting each other. The Woodhull Institute in San Fransisco found that men are going beyond the traditional shake and becoming more comfortable hugging. (You could say the hug shows you are entirely unguarded.) Still, men over fifty find it most difficult to embrace, except for Hollywood and ethnic groups. Gen-Xers are more comfortable giving a same-sex hug in a public place, other than a sporting field or arena.

The "Charlton Heston hug" of half handshake/half pat on back is a combination of the two that most men are willing to do.

Gerald Levin, former CEO, Time Warner, and Steve Case, then-chairman of AOL, sealed their deal with a hug. Former Vice President Al Gore celebrated his nomination-clinching primary win by turning from the microphone to embrace a prominent male backer. And, of course, you have former U.S. President Clinton, who "craved a hug from everybody."

Years ago one CEO told me that he always gives a hug to people he meets—even the ones he's meeting for the first time. They "relax and enjoy it, or are catatonic, but they never forget it." All I ask is that you try this and everything else recommended in this book for yourself. You might find people "relax and enjoy it and never forget it" from you too.

Stephen Largen, CEO, MacDermid Printing Solutions, says, "Coming from England it's a standoff country and you only give a stiff handshake. I've learned to give a pat on the back and people really respond to it. It's a connection." Well, that's a start.

The current twist on a handshake is a bump. A bump is two clinched fists up against each other, à la the Hewlett-Packard and Compaq alliance. It's a type of handshake that is a little too trendy for the rest of the country but that was an acceptable photo op between the female and male CEOs. Hugging would be a bit of a risk and the handshake too cool for the camera.

The bump will likely never replace the handshake. You can't imagine people "doing business on a bump basis," can you?

The air kiss or real kiss is another sometimes appropriate greeting. Attitude and technique is important. With Europeans you'll likely exchange an air kiss. The sequence in the United Kingdom is left cheek to left, then to the right. In France it is left cheek to the left, then right, then left again.

Whether real or in the air, if you don't want to be the recipient of a kiss, you don't have to be. A firm handshake, smile, and remembering the person's name can convey the same sincerity, trust, energy, willingness, and so on to do business together.

To receive any touch—a bump, handshake, hug, shoulder clasp—relax and respond with one back or at least with a relaxed smile. Don't wince, dodge, jerk away, glare, hit back—*if* the person has attempted to touch you with good intent and form. Don't for one second tolerate an inappropriate or lascivious touch. Don't assume; find out with full disclosure if it was. Then, right then and there, address the issue, while still giving acceptance, maintaining self-esteem, and having a relaxed smile on your face.

If you've consistently used full disclosure in what you want, it's natural to follow that up with more, "I like our good working relationship, Joe, but I don't want to air kiss when we meet." As you say it, smile, and grasp the person's shoulder. If it's the second time you've had to make this clear, grasp just a little too firmly.

Be consistent. If you're going to touch, which you obviously should, above all be consistent. Touch men and women, older and younger people, those up and down the organization, inside and out, regardless of race, creed, or color. Don't selectively go after the ones you're comfortable with, like, trust, or are attracted to. (That's where harassment can start.) As in acceptance, esteem, question, and favors: Everyone gets the same from you.

Diane Hartman, director, Veterans Administration Hospital, told me, "I always hug and kiss my son good night. When I travel I give a kiss and hug for every day I'm gone so he has them stored up. Then I give him an extra one or two for unknown situations. He's fourteen years old and if I forget, he'll remind me before I leave. I like that. He doesn't forget."

Consistency provides security for people in that they know what to expect: giving and expecting acceptance to maintain self-esteem.

The easiest to touch are the ones you're familiar with or have a shared experience with. If you are going to become familiar and have shared experiences, you might as well initiate a touch to get it going. You will get familiar and have a shared experience through the touch sooner! When I discussed this with one CEO, he commented that you see touch on the sporting field because of the shared emotional experience of winning or losing. He said, "There isn't a lot of hugging the first day a rookie shows up on the practice field. It takes time to develop the relationship." But how quickly would that rookie feel part of the team if someone gave him a welcome hug? Right away. You initiate to start the ball rolling in the sporting arena and in your life.

And when you do this, be sure to touch the scariest and most intimidating ones first. They are the ones others are afraid of too. They might be appreciative of your courageous connection, and you will set yourself apart from the rest in a positive way.

Just like in every one of the Sacred Six, someone you do this with might rebuff, reject, or flat out embarrass you because of your effort. When that happens, consider the possibility that it is done out of innocence and ignorance, not arrogance. Give the person the benefit of the doubt. Maintain your and the person's esteem as you ask for clarification about the response: For example, "Would you do me a favor and tell me how or why you reacted to the touch that way?" Adjust, connect, or apologize as necessary, but don't stop touching.

Count the number of times you touched someone today and go for more tomorrow and more the next day. Be consistent. Give the same good touch to the ones you know and the ones you don't. The ones you like and the ones you don't. The ones you'll see again and the ones you won't. You have to be consistent in giving touch so that you are trusted, liked, memorable, credible, and charismatic.

Don't overdo it. Just as in everything, good actions taken to the extreme become bad. It could be said that the "hugging president," Bill Clinton, took things to the extreme. But even people who proclaim, "I don't like to be touched" probably wouldn't have minded if the president patted them on the back and said, "Good job."

Good touch doesn't mean you go up to your boss and start giving a back rub with soothing words, "How are you doing today," even if he or she is stressed.

You have to use your good judgment; nonetheless, when in doubt, go ahead and touch. But do it right. Ask if there is misunderstanding.

Touch is about bonding with others—not just a physical tactile movement. A single friend of mine took a class on "how to flirt." The advice was to scope the crowd, pick a target, position yourself to be seen by the target, maintain eye contact, turn and face your target, and then touch yourself! It's as bad to touch yourself in business as it is touching others inappropriately.

One executive described a female's irritating habit, "She kept adjusting her hair when it wasn't out of place." When you touch yourself you look nervous, self-conscious, and invite thoughts of others' touching you! Refrain from touching your clothes, hair, and jewelry. In other words, don't preen or make sexual overtones.

Avoid touching around your mouth and nose, too. People concerned about germs will panic and avoid you.

Good technique includes good hygiene. You can't have your fingers in your mouth or nose and expect people to want to shake hands. You can't be playing with you ear and nose hairs then wipe your fingers on your shoulder and expect people to want a hug. Don't touch yourself, then others, unless you wash your hands in between. One celebrity CEO reportedly hands out towelettes before he shakes hands with people. (Like I said, anything good, taken to the extreme, becomes bad.)

"Germs are on elevator buttons, doorknobs, pens, computer keys. I use my shirttail or jacket end to open bathroom doors. And

I only use my knuckles on the elevator buttons, never my fingertips," says one lawyer. "Germs are everywhere and most people are disgusting."

The chairman of a company touched himself so much that out of curiosity I watched and counted the number of times. In less than three minutes he'd touched his face, nose, ear, and mouth twenty-six times. Someone else observing him asked me if I thought he was sending in a baseball play.

6

Slow Down, Shut Up, and Listen

A lot in this book has been about *doing:* your taking the initiative to ask questions, ask favors, use humor, touch, and smile. Part of doing is slowing down, shutting up, and listening. Remember, Executive Charisma isn't as much about you as about your effect on others and that comes not just from what you say and do but from what you don't say and don't do.

In the late 1800s Oglala Sioux, Luther Standing Bear, said, "Conversation was never begun at once, or in a hurried manner. No one was quick with a question, and no one was pressed for an answer. A pause giving time for thought was the truly courteous way of beginning and conducting a conversation. Silence was meaningful with the Lakota, and his granting a space of silence to the speech-maker and his own moment of silence before talking was done in the practice of true politeness and regard for the rule, 'Thought comes before speech.'"

Everything that you could do and say is not important to do and say every day. Leave some things unsaid so that people hear what you have to say.

The Romans have a phrase: *il dolce far niente,* or "the sweetness of doing nothing." Now I would never promote "doing nothing," but slowing down, shutting up, and listening is *not* doing nothing. It is eliminating self-sabotaging behavior of talking too much and not listening enough.

Seventeenth-century scholar Chang Chao said, "It is contrary to God's will to eat delicious food quickly, to pass beautiful scenery hurriedly, and to speak sentiments superficially."

SLOW DOWN

Slow down means take on a conscious comportment in your movement, action, reaction, walk, and talk. Take time to pre-think the effect you want. Take time to choose the words and action that support the effect. Purposefully deliver those words with corroborating significance in your physical demeanor.

That constant awareness of your effect helps you do more in less time and do better with less effort. People will give you more attention and pay more attention to you with your steady pace. If you take the time to rest and test, you'll be a lot faster.

"Speed will kill you. Unnatural velocity in pushing things through will bite you. Pure raw energy doesn't work anymore. You can't speed and be effective, you can only be efficient," says Michael Trufant, CEO, ConnectUtilities.com. "You have to sit, have to listen, and go through the process to do it right. Stop, analyze, and plan."

Stillness suggests confidence and a certain maturity. Speed suggests nervousness and immaturity. Most people don't know how they look when they speed around, and if they did, they wouldn't want to look that way.

"A man in a hurry is not the image you want to portray. A man on a mission, okay, but not a man on the run. Male or female, take a deep breath, several of them, slow down, and see if you can get the business to come to you," says Jack Falvey, founder, MakingtheNumbers.com.

Slowing down doesn't mean dragging things out, being tedious, being laggardly, moving at a snail's pace, or being sluggish, old, and tired-looking. Nor does it mean being stubborn, dragging your feet like a willful child, acting scared, or trailing behind. Slowing down means being purposeful and acting with awareness.

Set an example for your people. There is a good side and there is a bad side to the saying "The speed of the leader is the speed of the pack." You have to lead with proper pacing during critical times. You speed up as necessary and slow down too.

Frenetic behavior, quick judgments, fast talking, rapid walking, speedy eating, and instant comebacks can cause you to

- Come across as nervous, scattered, jerky, desperate, rushed, breathless, scared, fearful, worried (causing stress and heartburn)

- Appear overwhelmed by things and the surroundings

- Look inadequate

- Lack organization and thought

- Look dishonest

- Look as though you can't be or shouldn't be bothered

- Sound clipped, brusque, rude, or defensive

Unfortunately, people believe what they see. The term for it in psychology is *behavioral confirmation*.

I realize your great hurry comes from good intentions and the need to be three steps ahead of others and in more places than one. You're in a rapidly growing company or industry. Technology changes things very quickly. There are high levels of stress. The economy is far beyond your control. You have demanding customers/clients and fierce competition. And you have constant staffing pressures.

You can't allow those realities to alter the effect you want to have. You can still be alert, agile, eager, quick but in a deliberate, purposeful, thought-out looking and acting manner.

Your purposefulness makes you more effective than your speed. In bike racing, a rider who decides to take off fast and get ahead of the "pelaton" is immediately followed by other riders. If the rider eases up a little instead, he goes unnoticed until he ends up way ahead of others.

Slowing down helps you

- Look confident, competent, comfortable, cool, calm, collected

- Appear thoughtful, focused, and planned

- Stay in control

- Remain unshaken

- Seem relaxed

- Keep in the loop

- Be calm, contained, strong

- Develop gracefulness

- Show and give respect to others

- Be less likely to mangle your words

- Minimize suffering mistakes made in haste

- Reserve energy

"I used to make decisions fast. Now I always sleep on them. Haste leads you into trouble. When I don't take the time to think it out and later it turns out to be a mistake, I feel it's because it was made in haste. When I reflect, decide, and it still turns out bad, at least I know it wasn't done in haste," says Kal Zeff, CEO, Carmel Companies.

Slowing down causes you to speak more clearly because you can think before you talk—or look like you have. Kal Zeff's native tongue is Hebrew, so he deliberately chooses to talk slower and clearer to be understood well. The result is that everything that he says sounds thought out. People listen because they want to hear what will come out next. Because his speech is purposefully paced, they can grasp every word.

The actor Kirk Douglas speaks about his stroke and subsequent slow speech, "The thing I found is people listen more."

"I admire people who speak in a comfortably easygoing and welcoming way. One man I know is like that; he doesn't waste time but does have a different use of time. He speaks as if he has no care in the world *and* all the time in the world for you. As compared to me who talks 10 million miles a second. I'm so hyped it's not easy to slow down. It's like I have ants in my pants and I'm fifty-two years old!" said one executive.

HOW TO SLOW DOWN

- *Think, prioritize, and choose.*
- *Execute.*
- *Have a mnemonic device to keep you on track.*

Think, prioritize, and choose. Spend two or ten minutes sitting/standing (with Cheez Whiz and good posture) several times a day and think about what should be done next and how. It's shocking how much we do, do instead of think, do, think, do, think, do. When you think, observe, ask questions, and then prioritize and choose your action. Some things are more important than other things. Important issues get lost in the crush of the smaller ones. The need to act and act fast pushes out thinking. There is so much to do and so many options to choose—thinking helps you make the complicated simpler.

"My garden is my place. Before I get in the car and drive to work I stand in the yard and just look around and think. I'll stand there in the rain with my umbrella and briefcase for ten minutes sometimes, just looking and thinking," says Janice Aune, CEO, Onvoy.

The firefighter dictum is "Firemen should never run." It's important to stay calm, to size up the job before rushing in. And even when they rush in it's in an organized approach.

"My mind works fast and my mouth can't keep up. My mind and mouth have a race," says one CEO who's trying to slow down and think more.

One CEO told me, "I say everything to myself before I say it out loud so I'll hear how it sounds and change it if I need to." I asked, "Doesn't that take a long time?" He said, "Yes, in the beginning it did, but now I've trained myself to do it and it only takes a few extra seconds."

Gene Pope, vice president e-commerce platforms, Amazon, says, "To slow down I ask questions that cause people to think. It stops my rapid rush into action and presents a calm demeanor. I try to be calm in the face of the storm." Just as he asks questions to cause people to think, you can ask yourself questions to cause yourself to think.

When you choose and prioritize, you slow yourself down. Then you can slow down and breathe purposefully and deeply so as to make the words come out of your mouth clearer and better paced. Because the words are coming as you want in clear complete sentences, you feel calmer and more comfortable in maintaining eye contact. When your body moves in a sustained flow, you create a controlled calm around you and anyone else near you. You end up with fewer jerky movements.

Personal security experts say that in an aggressive group you should look for the slowed down, calm ones; they are the most dangerous because they are in the strongest position to take control as they look at the whole picture and take action accordingly.

A particularly important time to think and choose is in reacting. Fast acting and fast talking cause reactionary mistakes. If you are slow to snap back, react, and make quick judgment, you'll look confident, controlled, competent, cool, calm, and collected and minimize misunderstandings and problems. "When I make a judgmental knee-jerk response, negative energy wells up inside me. So I relax, breathe, rethink my response, and ask a question like, 'I don't fully understand. . . . Tell me more,'" says a CEO.

Jack Falvey says, "Being fast on your feet means you have to be even faster to bite your tongue before you do more harm than good."

"I stop and reflect on a decision and opinion before I make them," says Don Gulbrandsen, CEO, Gulbrandsen Manufacturing. "In a meeting, when a thought is burning in my forehead that I want to blurt out, instead, I write the thought down on a pad and I feel released. I can forget it for now and later email, mail, or voice mail it with a comment like, 'I observed this. . . . Did you see that also?' As the longtime CEO I can see problems and solutions quickly, but I've learned I need to let solutions unfold on their own with other people. If I answer one problem, then they throw all the problems my way. I become the one-stop problem solver and then people don't learn for themselves. So instead I get very quiet and write."

If you don't have time to think before you react, have your first response be a question. A question slows you down and buys you time in responding. Asking helps you prioritize, learn, and choose your course.

Execute. Hurry up and start slowing down. Think, then execute with purposeful, deliberate, aware action.

"Calm down, come down off your pedestal, don't put people down, and keep it down," writes Jerry Seinfeld in one of his children's books.

You can be quick, but you don't have to hurry. There's a difference. You get to where you're going faster and more effectively when you go at a fraction of the speed that you can. You cruise through things in an easygoing gracefulness. When you slow down you create a reserve of energy that you can call on when required.

One female executive said, "I slow down to command the room. Most women don't use this very often, and I've found it makes people curious to listen to you."

A human resource executive told me that she partially judges when people are ready for promotion by how they learn to slow down and take charge of their time. "In the early stages of a career if the person has to fly from New York to Los Angeles, I see him or her booking a flight with four legs. When the person figures out to book nonstops I know he's ready to move up. When she figures out how to get someone else to go for her, I know she's ready to move up."

As much as I promote slowing down, I also promote doing just the opposite—on purpose for a purpose. The best CEOs I know literally *run* into a meeting, up the stage stairs, around the car to get your door on occasion for a purpose. They could strut but they choose to "move out" and "hit the deck running."

You can be deliberate, prepared, and purposeful but still be energetic. One CEO says, "I do some things fast if they are boring, taking up my time, and because I want to be active and move briskly along. But I can also slow down when necessary."

So choose to move on purpose with a purpose. When you enter a colleague's office, walk down the street, scratch your forehead, repeat someone's name when introduced, answer the phone, leave a voice mail, and the rest.

Choose to slow down on purpose with attention to how quickly you release a handshake, get up from a chair, walk out of the person's office, and the rest.

Do whatever you do a little slower, a little calmer, with a little more awareness. (Kiss your significant other for a full four seconds. Seriously, try this one today.)

It's good practice to speak as if you're using an interpreter. Say something and let the listener translate it before you say more. Or talk to your boss as though you're talking to a five-year-old. Use clear, deliberate, simple words, with pauses put in, along with facial expression, to aid in understanding. You'll appear more well thought out. You make yourself easier to hear and be listened to.

Avoid doing two things at once (such as eating and reading or talking and typing or as I saw a woman in San Francisco do—walk down a busy city street as she was smoking and knitting). The fact that you can multitask doesn't mean you should.

Slow works well in many situations. Take something as straightforward as exercise. One journal reports that the latest trend is Super Slow Exercise. For example, lift weights as slowly as humanly possible then sit back and enjoy newfound muscles and weight loss. Lift excruciatingly slowly for ten seconds and lower the same for ten seconds. Being slow is far more difficult than it seems. Of 147 people in a study to practice Super Slow, only two lasted through the ten-week program. "The product is great but the process is painful" according to the sponsors.

Have a mnemonic device to keep you on track. You will need to catch yourself about seventy-seven times a day to pause, breathe, slow down, think, act. When you're busy doing, you can forget to remember.

Choose some device to cause you to Pavlovian-like register to stop, think, prioritize, and choose. Every time the phone rings you could remind yourself to slow down. Every time you pick up a fork, slow down. Every time that you see the color purple, slow down.

Professional photographers learn to wait for the right light, wait for the right facial expression. Whether it's the light, expression, or location, have the self-imposed discipline to slow down and not just snap.

Slowing down literally makes you safer out in public. I was in an elevator in San Francisco when the door opened for the floor another passenger had pushed. But the elevator wasn't in sync with the floor level; the floor was about nine inches higher than the elevator when the doors opened. Without looking, the man in the elevator with me hurriedly stepped out, whacked his shinbone on the uneven floor surface, and fell flat on his face.

PUBLIC SPEAKING

A good place to test your skill in standing straight, tall, smiling, and slowing down is in a group situation. It might be a Monday morning meeting, board of directors, or a PTA meeting. Regardless, you have to stand up in front of many eyes and speak to inform, educate, entertain, and get support for your cause.

When one CEO gives an important speech he plants people in the audience to spontaneously burst into a standing ovation, causing the rest to join in. And when he's on a radio or TV talk show, he has his people call in with questions he wants to answer. If you use these "dos and don'ts," you won't have to resort to "planting" people. Your audience will come to you on its own initiative.

Some dos and don'ts:

- Don't befuddle yourself with negative self-talk. Instead say, "I can do this and I can do it well."

- Do write your presentation with a strong opening; then expand the opening with the magic rule of three. (Three of anything is understood more quickly and remembered

continued

longer.) Support the "three" with stories that are personal, use interesting words, and include some sort of survival. (People like that. It doesn't have to be surviving the wilds of Africa but surviving a job termination, divorce, bankruptcy, mistake, etc.) Close with an extra powerful story. This can be done in a three-minute speech or a thirty-minute speech.

- Do keep it simple and to the point. Shorten whatever you plan to present. Begin with a specific end result. Do make a point and have the point be clear.

- Do rehearse. Practice your speech even if you only are going to have three or four people in your audience. Try on your material. Have more than one "try on" to eliminate self-sabotaging words and actions. By the time you actually give it, it should almost be second nature to you. It is a mistake to "wing it" without rehearsal.

- Don't follow the old (dumb) advice to imagine your audience naked; that will only make you nervous. Instead imagine them liking your presentation and thinking you are just superb.

- Do check your clothing the night before; make sure all the buttons are there. Rehearse in the shoes you plan to wear. Be careful wearing a silk blouse because lavaliere microphones can irritatingly pick up the sound of rustling cloth; the same can happen with a silk tie.

continued

- Do check weather in advance for possible flight delays. (Rolling Stones's Mick Jagger is famous for watching the weather and planning accordingly to get to the next location even if his band doesn't.)

- Don't eat right before you go on; belches, burps, food allergy manifestations, sneezes, and such get magnified with the microphone.

- Do get out from behind the lectern; your effectiveness will increase at least 200 percent. Speak bigger. Keep head level. Don't bounce, walk, and move around too much. Vary the distance between you and the audience, move in and out without a lot of back and forth. Make sure your physical moves corroborate with your verbal message. Obviously stand tall, straight, and smile.

- Do start out (and continue) speaking more slowly and more deliberately than you feel like doing. You look prepared for the audience. Keep a deliberate pace; don't speed up because you're running out of time. Instead cut. Don't go past your allotted time even if the speaker before you did.

- Do talk to the audience as though it's a group of old friends having an informative conversation—a "we're all family here" attitude and approach.

- Don't say words so fast that you stutter, and avoid too much repetition of the same word or expression. Eliminate "and-ah, ahhhhh, gunna." Watch your grammar and pronunciation.

continued

- Do phrase your words for sound bite attention. It takes good script writing and rehearsal of what you scripted. If you don't listen to yourself or listen to your audience, you won't do well.

- Don't tell too much and just talk and talk and talk. Slow down and give them time to catch up. Ask for audience reaction, input.

- Do be personal, detail-oriented, and concise. Try to include references to the audience about the subject to humanize your presentation.

- Do maintain a relaxed smile throughout, not an open, overly eager smile.

- Do turn up the juice; you'll get better reviews.

- Do use visual aids correctly. If you use PowerPoint get a light on your face simultaneously. I've seen numerous CEOs "in the dark" literally and seemingly figuratively by not having that extra light.

- Don't allow yourself to be scheduled to speak for 500 people when the room can accommodate 20,000. Avoid satellite transmission. Everything you say will have a split-second delay and make you look "slow minded," as if you need extra time to comprehend questions and form answers.

- Do be prepared to adjust and continue on if the power, lights, or sound system go out during a storm. Don't rely on technology.

continued

- Don't wear your lavaliere microphone into the restroom or in private conversations during the break. It might still be on.

- Do remember that you're "on" before you're on *and* after you're on. Gestures, posture, and movement are watched from the second you get out of your car and walk across the parking lot to the meeting room.

- Do plan for likely questions. Good Q&A is like having a conversation, so anticipate what might get asked and rehearse your answers.

- To handle questions (hostile and otherwise) first acknowledge the questioner's viewpoint ("I understand it may be frustrating . . .") Thank the person for bringing up the issue. State your opinion from your experience (no one can argue with one's own experience). Accept theirs but state yours too. Don't repeat the negative or use their emotionally charged words as you restate the question. Then answer.

Alternatively, ask about the question and throw it out to others, "Does everybody agree with that?" Hopefully they don't! If truly hostile questions keep getting fired at you, soften your voice, drop your gestures, take out the voice inflection (do the opposite of dynamic), and answer. It makes you look calm, cool, and collected.

And when you finish, it's a nice touch to add "Thank you for listening." Listeners feel appreciated and will almost always give a little more applause.

SHUT UP AND LISTEN

Be completely responsible for everything that comes out of your mouth. If you don't know exactly what to say, say nothing. Don't add to the noise pollution already in the world.

"Even if I don't hear what I like, I've learned that you let them get through it. I usually find you can't make your response heard if they feel you didn't listen to their complete message. I think to get respect, you have to hear them out. Once they get it out, they are more willing to listen to you. I need them to be as willing to listen as possible, in case they don't like what they are going to hear," says, Michael Trufant, CEO, ConnectUtilities.com.

Limiting your talk does not mean limiting your contribution. Say what is needed, but not what isn't. The good thing is that no one can hear what you don't say, and it can't get you in trouble.

Shutting up and listening doesn't mean being dull, shy, stubborn in contributing, nor is it giving up, pouting, clamming up. It's choosing to listen and think first rather than say and do. Like the Bible says in James 1:19, "Be swift to hear, slow to speak."

When you shut up and listen, you

- Contain your mental and physical energy instead of pouring it into a hundred reactions

- Pay more attention to what others are saying and doing

- Act like a thinking individual

- Have the time to formulate the right response

- Gain trust

- Avoid talking too much and putting your foot in your mouth

- Save yourself from embarrassment

- Maintain others' self-esteem

- Appear to be warm, sincere, and human

- Avoid hurting someone's self-esteem

- Be more personally powerful

- Avoid looking dumb

- Communicate in a universally understood language of silence

- Keep from doing an emotional mugging

As the saying goes, "A closed mouth gathers no foot."

You have to listen to others, not just to yourself. Take a deep breath. Lots of them! Shut off the part of your brain trying to formulate an answer and just listen to take in information.

Silence says many things in every language. One of the greatest sounds of all is the sound of complete silence.

HOW TO SHUT UP, AND LISTEN

- *Think, prioritize, and choose.*

- *Execute.*

- *Have a mnemonic device to keep you on track.*

Think, prioritize, and choose. Think what you might say. Think what you could get away with not saying. And say what is left. The hardest thing to say is nothing.

Prioritize the things you really should say and choose the time to say them.

One source quotes Queen Noor of Jordan recalling her life with her late husband, King Hussein, "I told him as little as possible of anything that might disturb him. He needed me to help alleviate the crippling burdens he had to bear, not to add my feelings of frustration or hurt or not knowing what to do. I tried to be as much support to him as possible, and I tried to deal with anything that concerned me on my own."

You don't have to share everything with others. You don't have to participate in constant verbal communicativeness. Not every thought must be expressed. You don't have to meet their stories with your stories.

Speaking less and listening more is still consistent with full-disclosure communication. You're clear and complete in saying the right thing in the right place. You don't say everything that could be said even though it's so tempting.

When you meet someone in the hallway, you don't have to get involved in incessant conversation, just wave and smile and go on. To cease talking is a fine way to end a conversation.

"Don't think you have to say everything. Everyone knows you're smart; you don't have to say it all," says Steve Largen, CEO, MacDermid Printing Solutions.

Make it easy for people to listen to you too. People will be willing to listen if you can explain why they should listen in ten seconds. (If there is something in it for them, they'll be that much more attentive.) In the next thirty seconds say more of what's in it for them.

Shut up, listen, and smile as opposed to dumping more info. Be direct. Be brief. Be gone.

Asking questions helps you prioritize and choose when you want to talk and when not. When you listen well, the questions you still need to ask become evident. Asking gives you an excuse to shut up, lets others talk, and yet provides the tool to interject in the conversation by asking another question.

One publication described Vladimir Putin's leadership, "Speak less, listen more. Don't say anything you don't need to say. Don't form hasty conclusions. If you decide, decide. Be underestimated. Calculate your responses."

Execute. Stop. Bite your tongue. Smile instead of talk. Ask a question. Count. Pinch your fingers into your palm. Listen. Lean in. Write what you hear. Repeat. Ask questions. Keep biting your tongue.

One company head told me, "I tend to take over a conversation, and I only shut up because I have to. Deep down I worry that if I don't talk a lot then I won't have a chance to talk. But when I do shut up and ask someone else I'm amazed what happens. They come up with something very important that I was missing."

Some people never have an unspoken thought. Most of the time whatever you've said, you've already said too much. If you say what doesn't need to be said or say the same thing too many times, people will drift off, lose focus, get agitated. As Ben Franklin wrote, "Speak not but what may benefit others or yourself; avoid trifling conversation."

Don't think out loud, it inhibits others' thoughts. Don't speak just to hear yourself, look smart, or draw attention to yourself for ego's sake.

One six-foot four-inch CEO said, "I listen by stepping closer, bending at the waist to lean in. Then I step back when I talk. It's very effective."

Set aside your opinions when listening. They get in the way of hearing. People don't want an answer when you're listening. What they want is empathy, sensitivity, and understanding.

"I have found that the best way to listen for me is to shut out everything else, and only pay attention to the person, and to the context in which the person is speaking. I have to shut out other people in the room and stop thinking about what everyone else is thinking at the moment, and just listen to the person who is talking," says Visda Carson, partner, Accenture.

A Taoist expression goes, "The wise person does not speak. The talented one talks. The stupid one argues."

Cyril Cocq, Ph.D., engineer, Altran Technologies, describes his boss in France, "He is the most impressive person I have met. He doesn't need to say who he is, you know he is someone important: he acts very carefully, in a kind of slow, purposeful movement. He is very careful of the words he says. He smiles at you and without cutting into your sentence he listens, listens, listens to you and takes a pause to think before answering you. It raises the importance of what you just said and makes you feel important." He went on to say, "People who act like I described are rare in France and the ones who are, are very important and impressive and unforgettable." They are rare in every country in the world.

When you ask and listen, don't sift through your mail, do any sort of paperwork, work with your handheld, or shift your eyes and attention away. Be an active listener with all your sense focused on them, not a doer-of-something-else.

Listen with your entire body. Do it from your heart, not just your head. Empty out your own thoughts, yearnings, desires. You don't hear when your mouth is moving. Listen for more than what is being said. Be a good listener even if you don't like what you hear. If you do all this well, you'll end up exhausted from listening so deeply. But like they say about exercise, "It's a good tired."

"Listening is the most potent talent of a leader, especially to what may be unsaid," says Cal Turner, Jr., CEO, Dollar General. Never miss a good chance to shut up and listen. Listen, don't judge.

Instead, when you do choose to say something, count from three to ten before you start speaking. Count steps or people or lights in the room. Force yourself to slow down and focus on what the other person is saying and then what you're going to say.

It's also a good exercise to keep count of how many times you use needless filler words (e.g., uh, huh, ah). Count what percentage of the time you actually talk versus listen. Count the number of times you catch yourself shutting up.

When compelled to speak, repeat. Repeat something the person said. It shows you heard and didn't just cease talking. It's particularly good to repeat some detail at a later date.

John D. Rockefeller disciplined himself to be a great listener to retain important information for later use. "He would repeat to himself over and over the important points made by others. . . . Each night he would also talk out loud to his pillow, reviewing the day's events and voicing concerns," writes Peter Krass, author of the *Little Book of Business Wisdom.*

Judiciously interject. Try not to interrupt, but when you choose to, make your point then give the floor back to the person talking.

You have to help people out sometimes. They just nervously blab away consuming their time and yours. Keep a gentle control of the conversation by interspersing comments to keep things on track, avoid rambling, and be attentive at the same time.

A "hummm" will often suffice. "Tell me more or give me an example" is very good too. Instead of long digressive explanations, try a firm glance, a touch on the shoulder, a slow, deep purposeful nod.

When someone proclaims "I heard you" they probably didn't. That is not a good interjection. That proclamation really means "I haven't the foggiest clue what you just said."

Have a mnemonic device to keep you on track. In the "heat" of the conversation you can get carried away and forget to rein yourself in. Have some device to get you to refocus. It could be a sound, a word, an item. I use a specific piece of jewelry. When I start getting carried away I catch a glimpse, or feel it and it registers to slow me down, shut up, and listen more.

One lawyer told me, "I literally pinch myself on the knee under the desk to focus and listen. Same thing if I'm talking too fast. It's a reminder, 'Hey, stop, slow down.'"

If you don't catch and correct, you'll fall back into old habits. It used to be a sign of listening to someone to pick up a pencil and start taking notes. But it's a different signal when you pick up your handheld and start checking email.

Speed listening is basically just picking out a couple of key words, following up on those, and hoping that you've guessed right—not a good thing to do.

"The first reason to listen is purely because you might learn something that you do not already know. Second, the information might be used as a reconfirmation of your belief. Third, and most important, respect for the individual. The Golden Rule applies here: Do unto others as you want them to do to you," says Chet Kapoor, vice president and general manager, BEA Systems.

"Nobody likes a know-it-all and I know all about that," says one honest person.

7

Completing the Puzzle

Now you know the Sacred Six. All six have to be done by you all of the time for you to achieve the objective of Executive Charisma: to gain effective responses from others by using aware actions and using considerate civility in order to get useful things done. Making these six a part of you will complete the puzzle for your personal and professional success. Now it's up to you to do it.

DO THE OPPOSITE

You've undoubtedly noticed a pattern in all six: To do them well, you're doing the opposite of what most people typically do. There is a simple, overriding rule that works for everything, almost all of the time. The rule is: In any situation you are in, intelligently observe what most people do (and what you'd typically do) and *don't do that.* Embrace the opposite or at least a variation of the opposite:

- Initiate when others won't.

- Expect acceptance instead of feeling undeserved or unequal to others.

- Give acceptance instead of judging.

- Ask questions even if you know the answer.

- Ask favors instead of do, do, do.

- Stand tall even when you're too tired.

- Smile when you don't feel like it.

- Show humanness versus reverting to your role.

- Use humor when things are serious.

- Touch when you're afraid.

- Slow down when you have a lot to do.

- Shut up when you have a lot to say.

- Listen when you don't want to.

You always hear this advice, "You have to do one thing extremely well in life to succeed." The one thing you should choose to do well is to do the opposite of what most people do.

For Executive Charisma, do the opposite. Go against the social norm without being weird or stupid. It's impossible to do something spectacular unless you do the opposite from the majority.

One executive said, "I always sit right next to the person I'm having the biggest problem with. I do the opposite of what they expect, it takes courage, and if there is a possibility of getting a solution, I'm closer—figuratively and literally in making it happen."

Doing the opposite isn't being stubborn, or obstinate. It's being

- Flexible, adaptable, open-minded

- Pleasantly disruptive

- Open to discovery in new territory

- Willing to avoid the obvious and do the unexpected

- Leery of and reticent to go along with anything that becomes popular

- Brave in doing something differently from the way you did it before

It's not that you or others are wrong and the opposite is right. It's just that a different approach will give a different outcome. Sometimes it's more important what *not* to do than what *to* do. And what not to do is what everybody else is doing or what you have been doing. At the least, doing the opposite gives you tremendous freedom and unlimited choice. As one CEO put it, "Once you get a reputation for being slightly different and direct, it's amazing what you can get away with."

When I wrote this rule, I also said do the opposite of what *you'd* typically do. This is not to say you are wrong now. But if whatever you are currently doing isn't working, then *maybe* you are wrong. Regardless, don't keep doing it.

Take a minute and think about a problem, person, or situation you've repeatedly had and answer these questions:

1. What was the situation?

2. What did I do about it?

3. When it didn't work out like I wanted, what did I do differently?

4. When that didn't work, what did I do differently?

5. When that still didn't work, what did I do differently?

A lot of times you get stuck on number 3 and go no further. Doing number 4 and number 5 is required. Do the opposite by varying your action then varying it again and as many times as necessary. There is never a right or wrong. There is always a different and another.

"Doing the opposite" is a great problem solver but also a great differentiator. Dave Hardie, managing partner, Herbert Mines Associates, says, "Yesterday I received five emailed thank-you notes from candidates for interviews I've conducted and one handwritten note. I picked up the phone and called the one who wrote the note and said 'I appreciated the time and effort that you took to write.' The instantaneous email is too easy and common and doesn't set you apart."

Doing the opposite helps your creativity. "With my kids we did backward days growing up. Starting with dinner for breakfast and later breakfast for dinner. It taught them to be more creative and not to do the obvious," says Gene Pope, vice president e-commerce platforms, Amazon.

Doing the opposite makes for more interesting compliments. "Praise the beautiful for their intelligence and the intelligent for their beauty," says a sage.

Doing the opposite makes for good humor. When Garth Brooks writes a lyric, "Long neck bottle let go of my hand," the humor comes from the "opposite" that is required.

Doing the opposite provides better ways to do almost anything. Here are some examples of opposite behavior:

"Manage against the cycle: When a situation turns tense, grow outwardly calmer; when things are going well, turn up the heat." —*Joe Torre, Manager, New York Yankees*

"The most effective managers follow simple advice that others ignore in troubled times: Be bold. Act soon. Move fast." —*Fortune magazine*

"The prevailing wisdom is that markets are always right. I assume they're always wrong." —*George Soros, billionaire financier*

"Everything I do in marketing is what nobody else does. No one takes the time and initiative to do it. When I get an order for a custom Western holster I acknowledge it by stating the day and time of day it will be completed and shipped. Then I always ship it a day earlier than promised." —*John Bianchi, founder, Western Gunleather*

"I try to see what people are doing so I can go in the opposite direction." —*Pat Kuleto, restaurant designer, owner of Farallon in San Francisco*

"Brush your hair with the opposite hand and you'll increase your number of brain cells." —*Associated Press reporting on recent research*

"Two roads diverged in a wood, and I took the one less traveled by. And that has made all the difference." —*Robert Frost, poet*

"No one is thinking if everyone is thinking alike." —*General George S. Patton, Jr.*

"He customarily gives away to charity ten times the amount he spends on himself." —*Item about Sir John Templeton*

"If you want to build a ship, don't drum up the men to go to the forest to gather wood, saw it, and nail the planks together. Instead, teach them the desire for the sea." —*Antoine de Saint-Exupéry, The Little Prince*

"You can't win without being completely different. When everyone else says we are crazy, I say, 'Gee, we must really be on to something.' The louder they say it, the more excited I get." —*Larry Ellison, CEO, Oracle*

"Good news is no news, no news is bad news, bad news is good news." —*Jim Morgan, CEO, Applied Materials*

"We thought making it hard to get to would make the festival more hip." —*Robert Redford, on why the Sundance Film Festival is in Winter Park, Utah*

"Every time I'd give him something to do he'd do it brilliantly and ask for more. We just kept giving him more and giving him more." —*Donald Rumsfeld on why Dick Cheney became his replacement for Chief of Staff*

I could go on and on with people using oppositional behavior to do better. When it's pointed out it makes so much sense. If you followed the "do the opposite" rule in every aspect of how you think, act, and relate, you'd end up with behavior that is the Sacred Six. If you slow down, shut up, and listen you have the time to think of the opposite to do in the myriad of moments that make up your career.

Society counts on the fact you do what most people do. The science of persuading people to go along with the crowd is pejoratively referred to as "being a lemming." It's officially called "social-norms marketing." People are allelomimetic: meaning your behavior is influenced by the behavior of people around you. If they laugh uproariously, you're more likely to do so also. If they panic, you're more likely to panic. If they drink a lot, you're more likely to drink more. For example, a study out of William Smith College found that students consistently overestimated how much alcohol their fellow students drank. In turn, these students drank more themselves in an attempt to meet their misperceived standard of normalcy—the social norm. Wouldn't it be interesting if the social norm in business was Executive Charisma?

To complete the puzzle you just have to be good at one thing. That one thing is deliberately, consistently, persistently doing what others don't and what you'd typically not do. That takes practice.

PRACTICE

Practice everything in this book until you die. Everything that I recommend will take conscious repetition for that long. Enhancement of your Executive Charisma doesn't come about because you think it's a good idea and you want it to happen. Behavioral change experts say that you have to repeat a move 3000 times before it becomes a habit. It takes practice to train and retrain yourself after years of doing things differently. And after you finally "get it" you have to keep at it. These skills are perishable—if you don't keep at it you'll lose them.

Just because a person has twenty years of experience doesn't mean that it's good experience. Sometimes it's just one year of experience repeated twenty times.

If you're at the same level you were last year, you'll get run over. Thomas Edison's goal was to produce a minor invention every ten days and a major one every six months. Edison was inventing things. You're inventing yourself.

Take one part of the six and do that one thing all day, all week, all month long. Then add another and repeat the cycle. Nothing happens with a creeping nonchoice. One person said, "I don't do nothin', and I don't start doin' until eleven o'clock." The problem with doing nothin' is you don't know when you're done.

There are 800-plus opportunities a day to seek out and create opportunities for you to use the Sacred Six. Some suggestions to get you started for this week:

INITIATE

- *Say the important but difficult things that need to be said before you're comfortable.*
- *Be the first to be pleasant to someone who wasn't to you.*
- *Be the first to ask questions and ask favors.*

EXPECT AND GIVE ACCEPTANCE TO MAINTAIN SELF-ESTEEM

- *Tell yourself "I'm adequate" when you talk with an intimidating person.*
- *Remind yourself that the person who has exhibited jerk-like behavior is adequate as a human being too.*
- *Compliment a stranger, family member, or colleague today.*

ASK QUESTIONS AND ASK FAVORS

- *Don't tell all that you know; ask what they know.*
- *Frame comments into questions.*

continued

- *Do a favor for someone and ask for one before you do another one.*

STAND TALL, STRAIGHT, AND SMILE

- *Lift your rib cage off your pelvis. Pull your stomach toward your spine.*
- *Don't divert your eyes when you're talking to someone you're uncomfortable with.*
- *Smile even when you're mad or sad.*

BE HUMAN, HUMOROUS, AND HANDS ON

- *Volunteer the story about your first job (first setback, first success, etc.) in a discussion with a colleague.*
- *Plan some spontaneity by repeating a funny line you heard on a show.*
- *Touch the person's forearm seated beside you at the chamber of commerce meeting. Use a two-handed handshake when you meet someone—a "hand sandwich" as one person put it.*

SLOW DOWN, SHUT UP, AND LISTEN

- *Stop whatever you are doing at the top of every hour today. Stand up, breathe, smile, and continue on.*
- *When you have three things to say, see if one will suffice.*
- *Be silent and focus on how far away you can hear some noise right now.*

Be doggedly determined to do something you're clearly bad at or uncomfortable with. Schedule it on your calendar. Pick an easy one to start and take on progressively difficult ones. You can do anything for a day, however hard. At the end of each day, note your progress so that at the end of many days you'll see something beautiful and fine.

Remember, there is no "practice life." This is the only one you or I have. To make it a spectacular one, you have to practice good technique in *this* one.

As they say in the Navy SEALs program, "The only easy day is yesterday." Don't hold anything back. Push it to the maximum. The more attempts you make at improving, the higher your odds of succeeding the next time. Nail the culprits that cause you to fail and repeat bad behavior. Jettison ineffective behavior. Vow to never take another move without total concentration. Then relax a minute and try again. You'll find a little practice goes a long way.

Raise the bar high enough so that you don't clear it every time. That only cheapens the experience.

It has long been established that the best way to learn a skill completely is to teach it to others. Start with your children, and then work into it with friends, family, and colleagues if you choose.

The longer you keep doing what you're doing in the same old way the more unlikely things will change. Author Stephen King's rehab doctors advised him, "Do as much as you can do, then do a little bit more." Good for rehab. Good for progress. One day will be your breakthrough day and it all will fall into place. You'll know, and it becomes one of those "Call my mother moments."

A key to Executive Charisma is to practice all of this when it doesn't matter because you'll forget it on the conscious level when under a stressful situation and it *does* matter. When you are under pressure, strategy and process are the first to go and it's the time they are needed the most. Only if you've practiced will your subconscious take over.

The good thing about practice is that once you *re*discipline yourself, change habits, and improve your skills, you feel worse going back to old habits and can't even do them sometimes.

Mental practice works as well as real practice. Among top athletes the winning edge comes from the brain not just the body. Research claims 75 percent of conditioning is mental. Tiger Woods makes a mental image of the ball rolling into the hole. Kristi Yamaguchi mentally rehearses her routine before stepping on the ice. Michael Jordan practices mentally before returning to the court.

Never go where your mind hasn't gone before.

Another type of mental practice is to *optimistically* take a negative perspective as one to role play. Popular psychology and self-help advice suggests that you must have a positive attitude as you visualize. However, a recent study shows that for some people a negative attitude about a situation gives a better outcome. Instead of a sunny upbeat strategy, the only thing that can bring them a sense of calm is directly contemplating negative outcomes. Imagine all the ways your plan will go awry. And map out ways to avert the catastrophe. The idea is to plan for things to go wrong and then plan to handle it versus being surprised and unprepared.

Whatever your preferred method of change is, just do it.

Every coach of an Olympic athlete makes sure that his or her charge spends time in the "mental gym." American diver Michelle Davison says, "Everybody is pretty much at the same level physically. The difference comes down to who can hold it together mentally."

If you have intense concentration, you stimulate the same neural circuits that actually doing it does. "What matters to athletes is that just a visual imagery activates the brain's visual cortex, so imaging movement activates the motor cortex," says Harvard University's Stephen Kosslyn.

When you rehearse in your head, make it interesting. See yourself walking through the hallways of an impressive new corporate headquarters building (after the corporate car has been sent for you). People meet you going about their purposeful way and with a salute in their eyes say, "Good morning, boss." You see the administrative assistant outside of the boardroom, and she unconsciously stands up to eagerly greet you with her own standing ovation and escorts you in. People in the room just stop talking when you cross the threshold. Not out of some false obedience but because they really want to hear what you have to say, take in what you're wearing, feel your presence, follow your lead, and take your thoughts to the masses. You feel as comfortable walking into that room as you do walking into your kitchen for breakfast. A synergy grows into a controlled combustion that charges you up and everyone in there. And you feel right with the world as you diplomatically go about your business in a kick-ass way.

What a contrast to dreading and fearing the board meeting as you trudge down the hallway, slink along the walls, shuffle your feet with your hands buried in your pockets so you don't have to touch anyone. People you meet avert their eyes and sometimes dodge behind a partition. The administrative assistant begrudgingly grimaces at you, doesn't extend any extra effort, and points to the room you have to go in. No one notices when you walk in. No one stops talking, looks your way, or cares that you're there. You look like a naughty child. As a friend said, "You feel as uncomfortable as meeting your live-in lover's parents for the first time at a black-tie event and you're wearing jeans with holes in the knees." What enthusiasm there is in the room drains like a spilled cup at Starbucks. It's a weekly meeting or a weekly beating. It's up to you.

So now's your chance for your own Executive Charisma!

There is a lot that I don't know, but I do know this: You can do more about your future than your past. It's never too late to find out what you *could have* been or *could have* done.

Whatever your age, it's time for Executive Charisma. Trust me; you'll have major regrets if you don't do it starting *now*. If the person you'll be in twenty years could talk to the person you are today, that person would say, "Thank goodness you started when you did."

The average age of a Rolling Stone is in the mid-fifties. (The average age of an executive at GM is only forty-eight.) As Rod Stewart says, "Being a rock star at fifty is all about how you carry it off." Your unique brand of Executive Charisma is all about how you carry it off whatever your age or position in life.

John McEnroe says, "It doesn't matter whether you win or lose, until you lose." With Executive Charisma, you can still do something about your "winning" starting today.

People like to say, "Have a nice day." Living the material in this book ensures that you do. This works if you work it. If you don't, it won't.

You can be a solid citizen and make good money without Executive Charisma, but you'll have a more interesting, fun-filled, worthwhile, and satisfying life with it. It is true what they say: Fulfilling your potential will cut into your sitting around time though!

There is no time-off allowed in Executive Charisma. You have to use the same consistency as the great dancer Rudi Nureyev did in his profession. He would "dance" everywhere—to the window, to the door, across the living room floor.

If you take "time off" from your "Executive Charisma dance," do it in the privacy of your bathroom.

If you're already *good* at your work and then you add the last piece of the puzzle, there is *nothing* you can't do. At the least, you will experience the peace of knowing you did all that you could. And you'll avoid the lament that Louis L'Amour wrote, "It is a poor man who stops shy of his destiny."

EXECUTIVE CHARISMA: SIX-STEP SUMMARY

1. Be the first to initiate.
   - Put your fears aside or at least out of the way.
   - Seize the moment; take some—almost any—action.
   - Be consistent.

2. Expect and give acceptance to maintain esteem.
   - Tell yourself, "I'm adequate."
   - Behave as though you are.
   - Keep at it even when you don't get it.
   - Give acceptance.
   - Think to yourself about others: "They are adequate."
   - Treat others as though they are adequate.
   - Keep giving acceptance even when others seemingly don't deserve it.
   - Maintain esteem—yours and theirs.
   - Consistently follow the Golden Rule.

continued

- Choose and control your perspective.
- Be optimistic, overall, toward yourself, others, and life.

3. Ask questions and ask favors.
   - Choose your words and tone carefully.
   - Keep them organized.
   - Volunteer information without being asked.
   - Ask: Would you do me a favor?
   - Keep it simple. Be specific.
   - Thank them.

4. Stand tall, straight, and smile.
   - Do with what you have.
   - Lift up, suck in, and breathe.
   - Decide to live the rest of your life with a healthy, poised posture.
   - Relax your jaw, keep your lips apart, and turn up the corners of your mouth.
   - Retain that expression all of the time.

5. Be human, humorous, and hands on.
   - Cease dealing role to role and seek affinity.
   - Do it when others don't.
   - Don't overdo it.

   Be humorous.
   - Seek out humor.
   - Practice it always: Do it before they do and when others don't.
   - Don't overdo it.

continued

Touch.
- Have the right attitude; use good technique.
- Be consistent.
- Don't overdo it.

6. Slow down, shut up, and listen
- Think, prioritize, and choose.
- Execute.
- Have a mnemonic device to keep you on track.

Listen.
- Think, prioritize, and choose.
- Execute.
- Have a mnemonic device to keep you on track.

Complete the puzzle.
Do the opposite.
Practice.

So now's your chance to create your *own* Executive Charisma.

Index

ABOUT THE AUTHOR

D. A. Benton heads Benton Management Resources, an executive development and career-counseling firm in Fort Collins, Colorado, with clients in eiighteen countries. She is the author of numerous books, including the bestsellers *Lions Don't Need to Roar* and *How to Think Like a CEO,* as well as *Secrets of a CEO Coach* and *How to Act Like a CEO.*

-